Pros and Cons

Nearly 200 years after his death, Thomas Jefferson's *Life and Morals of Jesus of Nazareth* – "the Jefferson Bible" – continues to fascinate. Tom Huening provides a fresh look at this remarkable document, skillfully guiding the reader with a grounding in history and biblical analysis. Anyone interested in the life of Jefferson, America's religious history or biblical interpretation will find this work invaluable. -- Robert Boston, senior adviser, Americans United for Separation of Church and State

Thomas Jefferson, one of the nation's founders and third president, took scissors to his Bible and cut out the miracles of Jesus. Thomas Huening, in "Thomas Jefferson's Bible" reproduces what Jefferson left intact. It's a telling collection of parables and directives that emphasizes Jesus' concern that his followers live by his example and teaching. Traditional church instruction creates an imbalance toward miracles and eternal salvation to such an extent that 'living' the Christian faith is lost. Jefferson presents a badly needed corrective, which, if heeded, would enable us to mitigate the deceit, racism, misogyny, xenophobia, and other prejudices that threaten our democracy.

-- Bruce Blackie, Presbyterian Minister, Author of the novel *2084*

Huening's *Thomas Jefferson's Bible* was well organized and enjoyably easy to read, but I choose not to accept the dismissal of God/Spirit miracles that identify the Jesus I believe in. -- Skip Giles, Texas. Navy and airline pilot and Bible Study Fan

I am not a bible reader yet found this short history of the Bible and of Jefferson's thoughts very illuminating. In America some organizations promote a national religion (*their* religion) rather than separation of church and state. Book bans in Florida, the prospect of government funded religious schools, questions about prayer at public meetings and in public schools, all raise questions about our religious freedoms. Huening's *Thomas Jefferson's Bible* deals with these issues dating back to America's founding. All men cannot be created equal if they don't have freedom of conscience and belief. A valuable contribution to ongoing church/state discussions. -- Carol Perusse, Spiritual but Not Religious

Subscribing to any account of documented history is an act of faith. Wherever you stand on the Biblical scale of "myth" to "Divine Truth" – Thomas Huening takes you on a thought-provoking course in 'rebellious Theology'. With an adventurous and open mind, this reading journey will transport you through questions of religion, your faith, and the history of The Bible. It will have you fact-checking your knowledge and questioning the current state of US politics. If you simply read and implement the summarized bolded commentary written by the author after each Jefferson Bible passage - you would get something out of this book that might help you change the world.

-- Jeannine Graff, Constitutional Conservative

Thomas Jefferson's Bible

Religious Freedom in America

Thomas Huening

Copyright © 2024 Thomas Huening All rights reserved.

No part of this book may be reproduced, or stored in a retrieval system, or transmitted in any form or by any means, electronic, mechanical, photocopying, recording, or otherwise, without express written permission of the publisher.

ISBN: (Hardcover) 978-0-9817341-7-0

ISBN: (Paperback) 978-0-9817341-9-4

ISBN (eBook): 978-0-9817341-8-7

Cover: Painting by Rembrandt Peale, Public domain

SC Pubs - Spiritual Choices Publishing, San Mateo CA

SpiritualChoices.com

Printed in the United States of America

Religious freedom was "meant to comprehend, within the mantle of its protection, the Jew and the Gentile, the Christian and Mahometan, the Hindoo and infidel of every denomination."
Thomas Jefferson

TABLE OF CONTENTS

Preface: 9

Introduction 13

Part 1: New Testament Bible 101 17

Part 2: Thomas Jefferson 101 33

Part 3: Jefferson's Bible 45

Part 4: The Jefferson Bible and Comments 57

Part 5: Praise and Criticism 179

Part 6: Conclusion 191

Appendix A. Gospel of Thomas 201

B. Jefferson: Well, Nobody's Perfect 207

C. What Jefferson Deleted 213

D. Much Credit, Many Thanks, and Recommended Reading: 215

Afterword 219

Acknowledgement 221

About The Author 223

Jefferson's Bible

Religious Freedom in America

The unexamined bible is not worth living.
(sort of Socrates)

PREFACE:

I've long gone where discouraged or forbidden, as well as (sometimes annoyingly) questioned the mores and faith of my elders. As a Catholic in my 20s, I saw the *Index Librorum Prohibitorum* (*List of Prohibited Books*) as an invitation. Not until much later in life did I counter the Catholic Church's advice to avoid the Bible—the very basis of Christian belief. I've since become fascinated by this all-time bestseller and began exploring its history. Among the many variations, I stumbled upon founding father Thomas Jefferson's *The Jefferson Bible*. I asked myself: What did this currently criticized, slave-owning, but "all men are created equal"-spouting third U.S. president have to say about the Bible and, most importantly, religious freedom?

I discovered, and you will too, his selective biases, as well as his presumption and touch of arrogance, as he imagined that he could improve the approximately 2000-year-old classic Bible, which is treasured by perhaps a billion human beings. I found that he had an underlying motive for not just creating his New Testament Bible, but in influencing his two other proudest accomplishments. His founding of the public (and not religiously affiliated) University of Virginia, his authoring of the Declaration of Independence, and his personal Bible rendition all rested upon his bedrock belief in the separation of church and state. He recognized that we all can be equal and free in government and education—only if the state and the church remain free from each other. He knew, too, that they would forever be inclined to join forces to control their subjects.

Aged 76, his reputation and place in history assured, Jefferson went where no man of his time and stature would go. He boldly edited and redacted the sacrosanct book of his era. Ostensibly for his private use, he preserved it by bequeath, intending it as an important reminder to a time like the present when "freedom of religion" has turned to the opposite: a call for reuniting church and state, which is really a call for a Christian United States.

Did Jefferson succeed? Yes and no. His Bible saw the light of day some 75 years after he died and created the controversy that he must have anticipated. He revealed his own biases by his personal, arbitrary choices of biblical passages to include or exclude. He certainly cemented and exposed his dissatisfaction with the myth, dogma, and the discrimination against rival sects and denominations of the essentially state-sponsored religion of his day: Episcopal and Puritan in most American colonies. He leveled a parting shot directed at the ongoing toxic marriage of the state and church.

Extraordinarily well educated, perhaps the quintessential Enlightenment movement man, he nonetheless knew less than he realized. He had benefited from perhaps 50 years of embryonic independent academic research on the history of the Bible and of the human Jesus. He couldn't yet benefit from the ensuing 200 years of continuing academic study and discovery. I'm no Thomas Jefferson, but even as a former Bible avoider, I've gained that information advantage by studying volumes of research and hope to share that academic knowledge in layperson's terms.

Discussion is the object, not proselytizing. I agree with Jefferson that your belief in 20 gods or no gods at all does me no harm. I happen to share Jefferson's belief in a deist-type god, one of nature, that's unlike the one presented in either the Old or New Testaments. I appreciate the peace and comfort that my family and generations for millennia have gained from Christian and other sacred scriptures. However, I believe we humans can be good without belief in the supernatural. I believe spirituality and perfecting our human state is an essential ongoing process.

This is my contribution to that ongoing quest.

Consistent with current academic practice, I refer to dates not before Christ (B.C.) and after Christ (A.D.) but as C.E. for Common Era, and B.C.E. for Before Common Era. Consistent with *The Jefferson Bible,* I deal only with the gospel and epistle portion of the New Testament (NT), not the Old Testament (OT) of Hebrew origin. Rather than footnote my research, I allude to the authors and titles in the text and end with a substantial bibliography for further reading and research.

Introduction

President John F. Kennedy considered Thomas Jefferson the smartest man in American history. He said of him: "Thomas Jefferson was a gentleman of thirty-two who could calculate an eclipse, survey an estate, tie an artery, plan an edifice, try a cause, break a horse, and dance the minuet." Jefferson was classically educated in Greek, Latin, French, English, and in Bible study from his early youth. He learned the origins of religion and the Bible and came to believe that gospel writers Matthew, Mark, Luke, and John had chronicled common early Christian beliefs—but not much about Jesus' life and his moral lessons. Jefferson perused Aramaic, Greek, and Latin Bible translations, noting that they inevitably contained editing and transcription errors. He further learned that these many versions had historically been used for clerical and political control—both for good and for evil.

Jefferson, in late 1819 or early 1820, 15 years after an inadequate earlier attempt, decided to finally right these perceived biblical wrongs. He cut up costly printed Greek/Latin, French, and English Bibles that he had purchased many years earlier. He kept only passages that he thought represented the unadulterated lessons and teachings of Jesus and glued them side by side onto blank pages. He had his cut-and-pasted manuscript printed and bound in a single red leather book. To guard his privacy and public legacy, he revealed his redacted version of the Bible to only a few trusted friends. Intending to not publish his work while alive, he consulted it daily for inspiration and comfort. After Jefferson died in 1826, his one-edition edited Bible remained privately in the hands of Jefferson's daughter, granddaughter, and great-granddaughter for years.

When discovered in 1895, his Bible was purchased for $400 by Smithsonian librarian Cyrus Adler. In 1902, Iowa Republican Rep. John F. Lacey had Congress appropriate $3,227 to print 3,000 copies for the Senate and 6,000 for the House of Representatives. For many years following, each new member of Congress was presented with a copy of *The Jefferson Bible*. It's now in the public domain and freely available on the internet.

So, just over 200 years ago, Jefferson attempted to rescue the essence of Jesus's valuable advice and demonstrated virtue, which he found in particular passages of his *King James Version Bible*. He extracted his favorite passages, deleting myths and many duplications. Enlightenment movement Jefferson embraced those Bible passages that he thought were justified by science and reason but jettisoned those that he thought contained miracles, dogma, and fantasy. He picked out the precious little he found about the real Jesus he admired and created his own private bible: *The Life and Morals of Jesus of Nazareth*, now known as *The Jefferson Bible*.

* * *

Today, legacy Christians exit church in droves and young people can't fathom the Bible or religion as pertinent to their lives. Why read or revisit *The Jefferson Bible*? As a former Bible avoider, I identify. But the Bible, a sometimes fantastical, redundant, and arcane book, currently sells 20 million copies a year, with *five billion* printed over time. The Bible used by Jefferson was the New Testament (not the Torah or Jewish scriptures) and is a collection of 27 books discussing Jesus's life, teachings, and first-century Christian events. Many Christians believe the books' epistles and gospels were written by Jesus's pals, the apostles. Although those writings are thought to be "inspired," none of the authors knew Jesus and all were written 20 to 70 years after Jesus died.

Whatever your religious or "none of the above" identification, you likely recognize that the Christian Bible influenced Western civilization. I'd been taught that being liberally educated assumes familiarity with ancient Greek philosophers, Shakespeare, literary masters, and, yes, the Bible. "Love your enemies," "turn the other cheek," and "good Samaritan" are but a few biblical examples that we can all appreciate regardless of our faith or affiliation. Church leaders, afraid we Catholic minions might misinterpret the text and fall into heresy, discouraged private Protestant-type Bible study, and as such I never encountered a family Bible. Not until well into middle age did I finally read a Bible and learn its interwoven virtue and advice and begin to see the variety of its uses.

"I swear to tell the truth, the whole truth, and nothing but the truth, so help me God." Most of us have heard, and some of us have spoken, those words with our hand on a Bible—and then sometimes have spoken the truth. As a kid, more than once to validate a questionable fact, I and others would "swear on a stack of Bibles." Adopted by U.S. courts from the British, the custom of placing your left hand on the Bible and raising your right hand implied that we would not lie with God (Allah, affirmation, or affidavit) as our witness. Lying in court after swearing on a Bible to tell the truth was punishable as perjury.

Elected officials are typically sworn into office with their right hand raised and left hand on a Bible (or now on an iPad or Kindle), promising to defend the Constitution—and sometimes they do. Winne the Pooh, the federal budget, or no book at all can serve as a substitute, since it's a common ritual but not legally required. Many now choose a copy of the U. S. Constitution. Others choose different texts. For one, Keith Ellison, who's Muslim and was elected in 2006, was sworn into Congress on an English translation of the Koran once owned by Thomas Jefferson.

Can we share a shudder hearing a candidate claim how the "the word of God," the Bible, or some message from God directs them to run for public office and/or take specific political action. We've lately witnessed attempts to install the Bible as an absolute moral guide to our democratic government. Jefferson knew the negative results of church/state alliances: that is, the theocratic becomes autocratic.

What possessed Jefferson to write his Bible digest? Fundamentalist Christians would insist that the devil made him do it, while humanists would say that he was possessed of reason. Skeptics would say that he didn't trust organized religions' bible or the permanence of the wall between church and state.

Part 1: New Testament Bible 101

Early in his 30s, the Jewish Jesus followed and then stepped in for the beheaded John the Baptist. Itinerant proselytizers, they were just two of many in this turbulent historic time. John, more of a desert rat, and Jesus, who was more prone to hanging with sinners, lived poor and ascetic lives in a Jewish minority in a Roman-controlled world. Guided by the Hebrew scriptures, or the Old Testament to Christians, they preached repentance from sins and warned the wicked of the looming judgement day. They prophesized the return of political dominance and the future Kingdom of God to Jews, the "chosen people." Both populist preachers railed against the abuses infecting their beloved Judaism, and they especially criticized the ritual/legalistic hypocrisy of their Roman-installed and -controlled Jewish religious leaders—the scribes and Pharisees.

Unlike historic Jews, John the Baptist, Jesus, common folk, and pre-Rabbi Jewish religious leaders who were part of the Pharisees began to believe in an afterlife. Like many of the often-conquered Jews of the time, they saw God returning to judge the living and the resurrected who are worthy, as well as to restore an Eden-like kingdom on earth with a physical, not spiritual, afterlife. In that foreseen realm, the living and formerly dead would be judged according to Moses-inspired Hebrew scriptures. Those deemed evil would cease to exist and the just and holy would be rewarded with God-ruled Judean paradise on earth.

Jesus urged his fellow Jews to quickly repent for the maybe-not-the-end-of-the-world-but-coming-soon earthly

Kingdom of God. He struck a chord with the poor and dispossessed who could at least hope for a better life. Fearing political discord and bowing to the pressures of the Jewish high priest and Pharisees to eliminate troublemaker and public threat Jesus, the Romans tried and executed Jesus for treason. After having been crucified as a common criminal, his disciples first ran for cover, then thought that this couldn't be. To them, Jesus *was* someone special and his message had to live on.

And so, God resurrected Jesus. No, wait, he resurrected himself as the *son* of God, which, of course, means that he *is* God. Surely, therefore he couldn't have been common born but must have been born of a virgin in fulfillment of Jewish prophecy. According to Bart Ehrman in a 2001 *Los Angeles Times* Easter op-ed, Jesus's followers believed that his body had been brought back to life, signaling that the promised resurrection of all people from the dead had begun. Soon, then, both the living and dead followers of Jesus would be saved and inherit the promised Kingdom of God on earth. When that kingdom failed to appear, the timeline was sequentially extended, ultimately reaching the end of time.

When fellow orthodox Jews failed to accept the Jewish Jesus as the Christ, or the Messiah, his disciples turned to proselytizing outside of Judaism. Converted from Pharisee to Christianity, Paul of Tarsus superimposed prevailing Plato Greek thought onto Jesus's teaching. He led those gentiles to believe that Jesus must not have meant an *earthly* Jewish kingdom of man, but rather a *heavenly* kingdom of God. These converts came to imagine a spiritual, non-bodily second coming and judgement involving only their souls being judged and being then assigned to a not-on-this-earth eternal "heaven" or "hell." In *Heaven and Hell*, UNC professor Ehrman says that this wasn't the belief of Jesus or his original apostles. But by the end of the first century, and reinforced by John's gospel, this surviving soul concept became standard belief and remains central to Christianity.

Word spread and, as always, the story grew. Some 20 years after Jesus's death, zealous Jewish convert Paul proselytized far and wide, and Mark recorded the hearsay word on the street, which was then copied and enhanced by Matthew and Luke. Decades later, final gospel writer John sealed the *divine* side of the deal. Once it became apparent that the expected "end" wasn't happening in their lifetimes, many others joined the documenting efforts to ensure that Jesus's oral message didn't get lost. According to John Barton's *History of the Bible*, those early gospels at first were important "occasional literature," but only gradually developed into commonly accepted scripture early in the second century. He noted that early Christians didn't see Jesus's teachings as needing to be exactly copied so that New Testament manuscripts varied greatly and "none is authoritative."

In those early Christian times, many Bible versions existed until 303 C.E., when Emperor Diocletian attempted to burn all Bibles and bring Christianity to an end. He failed as sure as one emperor follows another. Then, in 313 C.E., the Edict of Milan permitted the practice of Christianity and allowed Bible ownership again under Roman rule. In 325 C.E., Emperor Constantine, to unify his empire as well as the Church, invited Christian bishops to Nicaea. He got them all on the same biblical page, which was then summarized by the Nicene Creed that's still used today: "I Believe in God the Father Almighty, Creator of Heaven and earth..." Christianity became the official religion of the Roman Empire when Emperor Theodosius I issued the Edict of Thessalonica in the year 380 C.E. Official New Testament Bibles currently exist in much that same form, but with myriad variations. We have no original epistle or gospel texts, only variants.

Many Christians, even today, consider the Bible to be divinely inspired or to be an inerrant account of the life and works of Jesus of Nazareth, his death by crucifixion, and resurrection from the dead. The New Testament Bible consists of epistles (letters) written by Paul of Tarsus and of gospel writings by Matthew, Mark, Luke, and John. Paul wrote his epistles between 48 and 60 C.E., some 20 years after Jesus's death, and scholars believe that Paul never knew Jesus before the latter's crucifixion. Some say that the gospel of Thomas dates to this time, others to much later.

The New Testament Bible contains four canonical (church-official) gospels written between 66 and 110 C.E., whose authors were anonymous. They were not eyewitnesses, and all reported common oral sayings—which is to say, hearsay—attributed to Jesus. Mark wrote first, followed and copied independently by the authors Matthew and Luke. They both drew on material from a presumed collection of Jesus's sayings known as the Q source, or Q, and other unique sources. John's gospel, written some 60 to 80 years after Jesus's death, reflected but didn't copy the writings of Mark, Matthew, and Luke.

The four canonical gospels do share the same basic outline of the life of Jesus: he began his public life after being baptized by John the Baptist; he referred to his followers as disciples; he taught in parables (short allegorical moral stories); and he healed the sick. He confronted and attempted to reform the corruption and abuses of the Roman-sponsored Jewish Pharisees and their other religious leaders. Accused, condemned, then convicted of treason by the Romans, he was crucified as a common criminal, and except for what's written in the early gospels of Thomas and Mark, he was said to be raised from the dead.

      Each subsequent gospel writer after Mark added to and enhanced the resurrection story, which ultimately became essential for the newly formed organizational church. To justify clerical leadership, the Apostle Peter (though really it was James, Jesus's brother) was anointed the official head of the Church and successor to the by now considered divine Jesus. The epistles and these four key gospels all reflected the points of view, times, and different theologies of their authors, like the non-official gospels of Thomas, of James, of Mary, and as many as 20 others. Jesus and his followers spoke Aramaic and possibly some Greek but were not writers and, in any case, believed that the end was near and apparently thought that a written account wasn't needed. Therefore, we have no direct quotes from Jesus in the Bible, and not until from 20 to 70 years after Jesus's death were the New Testament gospels written.

      Throughout his teens and 20s, Jesus and his fellow "God-chosen" Jews were expecting to escape the Romans' historic chains of oppression and subjugation—if only they would follow the sacred Hebrew scriptures and perform those rituals prescribed by their religious leaders. Except Rome had conquered and presently ruled the Jews and most of the then known world. Their Judaism religion had begun to ring false. Jesus condemned and threatened those Roman-sanctioned Jewish religious leaders for their show rituals and hypocrisy. He advocated for restoration of the kingdom of man and for Jewish freedom from imperial rule, actions which the Romans saw as treason, and which ultimately got him executed.

First ignored, then persecuted, then coopted by the state, Christian leaders formalized doctrines and dogma from Paul's epistles and the four gospels in the New Testament Bible—formalized by Emperor Constantine in the year 325 and ending for Jefferson using a 1769 revision of the 1611 *King James Version Bible*.

Jefferson's cut-and-paste version of the New Testament had a long-checkered history. Contrary to a few fundamentalists who believed that it fell from the heavens in current, completely edited English form, early Christian history began with B.C.E. Greek translations of the Hebrew Bible called the *Septuagint*. That was followed by the *Vetus Latina*, biblical manuscript texts translated to formal Latin. In 382, scholar Jerome, working from already corrupted versions of Greek, Hebrew, and Aramaic texts, and faulty Latin translations, created the common *Latin Vulgate*. The state-sanctioned Pope Damasus promptly designated it official, making it the most lasting and influential Bible in Christian history. Hand-transcribed down through the ages, with subsequent compounding errors, the 76-book *Vulgate Bible* was officially mass printed in 1590.

According to Lori Anne Ferrell, a Fellow of the Royal Historical Society, there are no originals of the books of the Christian Bible. Since its beginning it has "been endlessly trimmed and expanded, refashioned by its readers to meet the needs of religion, politics, and popular demand."

Luther mass published his *German New Testament* in 1522, but the first mass-printed English version was the 1526 *Tyndale Bible*, a New Testament translated from Hebrew, Greek, and the Latin *Vulgate*. In 1535, Myles's *Coverdale Bible* supplemented Tyndale's translations, creating the first combined Old *and* New Testament Bible printed in English, becoming the *Great Bible* in 1539. In 1560 came the Protestant *Geneva Bible*, the first authorized Bible of the Church of England. Then came the *Bishop's Bible* in 1568. In January 1604, King James appointed Richard Bancroft to revise this *Bishop's Bible*, consulting the *Matthew, Cloverdale, Whitechurch,* and *Geneva* Bibles. King James instructed translators to ensure that his new version would confirm to the ecclesiology, and that it would reflect the Church of England's belief in an ordained clergy and its leadership role in salvation and discipline.

This made-as-instructed 1611 *King James Version Bible*, a questionable translation from many prior questionable translations, soon was carried to the American British colonies. From 1619, the Church of England dominated the cultural, political, and especially the religious environment throughout the colony of Virginia. After a Protestant Evangelical revival of spirituality and religious devotion called the First Great Awakening in the 1730s and 1740s, Methodists, Catholics, and especially Baptists struggled as second-class citizens and unfairly paid taxes to support state-sanctioned Anglican ministers. Non-Anglicans couldn't serve in government and often were persecuted.

Between 1768 and 1774, Jefferson, in his late 20s, witnessed about half of the Baptist ministers in Virginia jailed for preaching. In reaction to the excessive piety and oppression of Anglicans, many people drifted away from adherence to the *King James Version Bible*, turning instead to atheism, Deism, and Unitarianism. Jefferson, though part of the favored religious class, noticed the unfair treatment of other religions and the general negative effects on individual freedoms. Also aware of the nascent Enlightenment scholarly efforts to uncover the historic *human* Jesus, Jefferson saw the resulting disconnect from the traditional Bible's *spiritual-Jesus*. That demystifying search effort continued, and much has been learned by historians and biblical scholars in the ensuing 200 years.

The New Testament, then and now, per Dr. Carl Krieg in a November 2022 essay, reveals an astounding contrast between what Jesus taught and what those later first-century gospel writers taught. A transformative and prophetic movement transitioned to a reactionary religious organization that still exists today. The church perspective at the end of the first century was quite at odds with what the initial disciples themselves proclaimed. Wives, be submissive to your husbands. Slaves, be submissive to your masters. Everybody, be submissive to the authorities. Fear God and obey the emperor.

Bible historians virtually all agree that no gospel author knew Jesus and that their writings were informed by hearsay, verbal accounts. Almost all now consider Mark's account as closest in time (after Paul's epistles and perhaps the gospel of Thomas) to Jesus's death. Again, no contemporaneous records exist; neither Jesus nor his disciples wrote anything. Mark, more than 30 years after Jesus's death, with the least editorializing, reported commonplace stories of developing Christian lore. For Mark, Jesus is a clearly *human* figure who sharply distinguishes himself from God.

In *History of God,* Karen Armstrong calls Mark's gospel the most reliable and "presents Jesus as a perfectly normal man, with a family that included brothers and sisters. No angels announced his birth or sang over his crib. He had not been marked out during his infancy or adolescence as remarkable in any way."

Gospel writers Matthew and Luke copied Mark and added from the hypothetical Q source. John then wrote more than 60 years after Jesus's death, completing the New Testament's evolution of Jesus from human to divine, writing to substantiate Jesus as the Messiah, the Christ, and Son of God. John also reassured the Christians of his time. Indeed, each evangelist wrote to a particular society that read the accounts in the context of their day. Most believers failed to notice how each of the four gospels offered an alternate picture of Jesus and his teaching.

In Jefferson's day, the Christ of early Christian teaching was no longer viable to those who had by then seen the heaven's planets and stars through Galileo's telescope. To Jefferson, Copernicus's astronomical work pointed to there being no resurrection, and that Jesus didn't ascend to the heavens *above*. It had become obvious, as in the ancient writers' common practice, that evangelists as storytellers had invented lines for Jesus to speak, enhancing his status as cultic hero.

Biblical scholars, in the 17th and 18th centuries during the Enlightenment, or Age of Reason, took up the challenge of the search for, as noted in *The Five Gospels,* the "Jesus behind the Christian facade of the Christ."

Jefferson, consistent with philosophers and Bible experts before and during his time, recognized that gulf between the historic and the biblical Jesus. So, finally, late in life, he cut passages from each gospel from multiple copies of the 1769 revised *King James Version Bible* and pasted them into his own one-edition book, which became *The Jefferson Bible*.

Here is a brief summary for each evangelist author, including details about the time and place of a gospel's composition and its points of view.

Gospel of Mark

The Gospel of Mark is the first of the four generally recognized gospels to be written, between 66 to 74 C.E. It likely collected oral accounts from Jesus's one-year public ministry. By custom attributed to Mark—thought to have been a disciple of Apostle Peter—it was actually written by an unknown author since no gospel writer knew Jesus. Although gathered from hearsay some 40 years after Jesus was killed, this gospel, which comprises about eight percent of the New Testament, is seen as the most authentic, since later gospel writers Mathew and Luke copied him, and John wrote even more years after the historic events. Per the Jesus Seminar's *The Five Gospels*, "Mark is now understood to be the fundamental source for narrative information about Jesus. The priority of Mark has become a cornerstone of the modern scholarship of the gospels."

Mark apparently believed that Jesus had ordinary human parents and an unremarkable birth, and his account begins with John the Baptist baptizing 30-year-old Jesus and declaring him a son and emissary of God. Mark tells us that

Jesus gathered 12 disciples and told them that he must die, but that he will rise again. He has Jesus first honored entering Jerusalem but then betrayed, condemned, and crucified. Mark's original account ended at chapter 16, verse 8, and Jesus's post-resurrection appearances were likely added by a later writer or editor. This gospel was written in Greek and for a gentile audience—challenging them to act and convert to Christianity according to Rev. Dave Rogers in his 2019 *The Difference Between the Four Gospels*.

Gospel of Matthew

The Gospel of Matthew was written circa 80 to 90 C.E., and also in Greek by an also anonymous author, who copied both Mark and the hypothetical Q source. Attributed to the Apostle Matthew, the gospel ascribed words to Jesus consistent with common Christian beliefs of his time and introduced Jesus as the Messiah forecasted in the Hebrew Bible. This gospel, which comprises about 13 percent of the New Testament, added birth, brief childhood, and resurrection narratives to Mark's account to demonstrate Jesus's divinity. For example, in Mark there is a young man at Jesus's tomb, and for Matthew that figure becomes a radiant angel.

Matthew's is the most Jewish of the gospels, seeking to convince orthodox, first-century Palestinian Jews that Jesus fulfilled the Hebrew Bible's prophesies that Jesus was the promised messiah. In a culture where patrimony and lineage were paramount, the gospel did cartwheels to establish Jesus's birth credentials. It also includes the account of the infant Jesus's flight to Egypt, conforming to the prophecies of Jewish scripture. No feminist or mathematician, Matthew had a post-partum Mary travel 40-plus miles on a donkey to escape danger, stay three or four years in Egypt, and return 100-plus miles to Nazareth after Herod died in 4 B.C.—*all before or at the time he said Christ was born.*

The Gospel of Matthew became the most important of all gospel texts for first-century Jesus disciples and second-century Christians because it provided a useful transition from the Christian designated Old Testament (Hebrew Bible) to what was deemed the New Testament. Church leaders needed to establish a connection to and a fulfillment of the Covenant of the Jews. Matthew emphasized the new religious order by having Jesus criticize the old order in an uncharacteristic and likely inauthentic way. Per Karen Armstrong in *A History of God*, "Jesus is made to utter violent diatribes against the 'the Scribes and Pharisees,' presenting them as worthless hypocrites."

Matthew ranked first in bible order due to elements important to the early church, such as his story of Jesus's miraculous conception and accounts of Jesus's life preferred by church leaders, including Jesus' death and resurrection. Matthew stressed the importance of teaching and discipleship, so his gospel fit nicely into the aims of early church hierarchy and clerical control. Later it fit with state unity and political control of Emperor Constantine's Council of Nicaea.

Gospel of Luke (and Acts of the Apostles)

Comprising around 14 percent of the Bible (27 percent with the Acts of the Apostles included), the Gospel of Luke was written between 85 and 110 C.E. and attributed to Luke the Evangelist, whose sources included Mark's gospel, the hypothetical Q source, and other sources. He provided accounts of Jesus's birth in addition to his early life, ministry, death, and resurrection. His later Acts of the Apostles described God's plan for world salvation, expounded first-century Christian history and early church growth, and described Jesus's ascension to heaven.

Some early fellow Jews accepted but then rejected the Christian message of Jesus as the Messiah (Greek *Khristós*, anglicized as Christ). Paul of Tarsus, after being converted to Christianity on his way to Damascus, took his Paul-spun message to diaspora Jews and non-Jew gentiles. Luke supposedly travelled part way with self-anointed missionary Paul to spread the word widely in Asia Minor. Luke wrote a more literate biblical account of Jesus for educated gentile Greeks. Fifty years after Jesus's death, Greeks cared little for Hebrew Bible prophecy stories and accepted Luke's rendition of Paul's version of Jesus's teachings.

Gospel of John

Written anonymously in Greek from 90 to 110 C.E., this gospel is attributed to John the Apostle, whose sources were only somewhat related to the prior three gospels, with his stated intent being "that you may believe that Jesus is the Christ, the Son of God, and that believing you may have life in his name." John wrote not about Jesus the teacher, but rather all about glory to a spiritual Jesus as God.

Some the vocabulary and ordering of incident contained within this gospel suggest that John knew of Mark and Luke's gospels but wrote independently of them. He also quoted Hebrew scripture, as did the earlier three gospel writers, but his quotations didn't exactly match any of their versions. He differs from the earlier three gospels, more echoing Paul's epistles: He writes of a self-described God, not of a historical human Jesus. All writing by John and others of his time suggest a common culture and are focused on devotion to Jesus as God.

The Gospel of John comprises 20 percent of the New Testament, and 90 percent of it is exclusive to John. He omits Jesus's ancestry, birth and childhood, and baptism. Jesus's ministry takes a single year in the other three gospels, but in John it's three years, and he has different dates for the crucifixion and the cleansing of the Temple. John uniquely tells of Jesus's turning of water into wine, the raising of Lazarus, the calling of the 12 apostles, the Sermon on the Mount, and Thomas's doubting of the resurrected Jesus. In a world then hostile to Christianity, John proclaimed Jesus as God to reinforce those committed to the church that John founded and led.

Gospel of Thomas

Not discovered until 1945 near Nag Hammadi, Egypt, among a group of books known as the Nag Hammadi library, this gospel is believed by scholars to have been composed by Christians as early as 50 C.E. and as late as 100 C.E., and only later honorarily attributed to the Apostle Thomas. Different than the four official gospels, it's a collection of sayings or teachings not unlike the hypothetical Q source. Jesus's early followers borrowed from contemporary sages and from popular culture to add to the status and legacy of their teacher. The Mark, Matthew, and Luke gospels contain 13 of the 16 Thomas parables. However, the Thomas gospel makes no mention of Jesus as a messiah, nor of his crucifixion, resurrection, or of a final judgement. According to *The Gospel of Thomas: The Hidden Sayings of Jesus*, by Marvin W. Meyer and Harold Bloom, the gospel reveals no fulfillment of prophecy, announces no apocalyptic kingdom, and Jesus dies for no one's sins.

Dr. Carl Krieg of *Progressing Spirit* says that the Gospel of Thomas suggests that there may have actually been 25 or more apostles and that the Thomas gospel represents their memories. Since this "sayings" gospel contains nothing about the crucifixion and resurrection of Jesus, he concludes that this group beyond the traditional 12 apostles knew little or nothing of the manner of Jesus's death or thought it to not be relevant.

According to the Jesus Seminar, the sayings in this gospel are actually or probably spoken by Jesus, and they're included in various forms in the other four gospels quoted by Jefferson. Those Thomas gospel sayings are listed in the appendix.

Epistles of Paul (not included by Jefferson)

Paul was a self-described zealous persecutor of Jesus's disciples, when in 33+/- C.E. he converted from being an orthodox Pharisee Jew to a follower of Jesus. As a fanatic missionary, and a repressed homosexual according to bishop and social activist John Shelby Spong, the self-ordained, so-called apostle Paul traveled the Middle East. Across what is now Turkey, Macedonia, and Greece, he converted and formed congregations of predominantly non-Jew gentiles. His initial sermons and teachings are lost but, from 48 to 62 C.E., he wrote follow-up, finger-wagging scold letters attempting to keep these early Christian congregations true to *Paul's* idea of Jesus. Given his spin on Jesus's teachings, it's a marvel that the resulting religion isn't called *Paul-ianity*.

According to scholars, Paul's letters comprise about a quarter of the modern Bible. Those letters were written closer in time to Jesus's death than any of the gospel writings. Paul followed Plato's ideas of immortal souls and turned Jesus's earthly message into a mystical one. Paul describes the *physical* resurrection of Jesus, that "Christ died for our sins in accordance with the scriptures, was buried, and *was raised*, appeared to Peter, to the twelve, to five hundred brothers and sisters, to James, to all the apostles and to me." Paul claims that if Jesus hasn't been raised, Jesus's message and our faith isn't credible.

Some of Paul's contributions to literature include: "all things to all men," "through a glass, darkly," and "When I was a child, I spoke as a child, I understood as a child, I thought as a child." One supposed Paul epistle, "Love is patient and kind; love is not jealous or boastful; it is not arrogant or rude…," is likely by a later author and has become a classic wedding saying.

Part 2: Thomas Jefferson 101

Third president of the United States Thomas Jefferson is best known as the author of the Declaration of Independence. Slightly less known is that he supported the revolution and that he was Virginia's second governor. He was also a lawyer, architect, husband, and father. Late in life, as a minor theologian, he created his own Bible.

On April 13, 1743, Jefferson was born on a central Virginia plantation to a surveyor father, Peter Jefferson, and a socially privileged mother, Jane Randolph. Education in Jefferson's early life meant devotion to four R's: Reading, wRiting, aRithmatic, and Religion. He started English school at age five and began Latin school at age nine, studying Latin, Greek, and French under a Scottish Presbyterian minister, Reverend William Douglas. When Jefferson was 14, his father died, after which he inherited a 5,000-acre estate that included the family home.

Early in 1758, Reverend James Maury began schooling Jefferson at a classical school for boys. After two years, Jefferson entered the Anglican College of William and Mary in Williamsburg in the spring of 1760 at age 17. At the college, students were required to be church members and professors had to declare adherence to the Church of England. In 1762 Jefferson graduated from William and Mary, began training by George Wythe in the law, and after being admitted to the General Court bar, he tried his first legal case in 1767. Jefferson also served as a vestryman in his local parish and was elected in 1769 to the House of Burgesses, the elected representative element of the Virginia General Assembly. Again, he was required to adhere to the state religion of Anglicanism, and to church doctrine and presumably the Bible. He had been steeped in his state's religion.

Jefferson married Martha Wayles Skelton in January 1772, and they would go on to have six children together, but only two survived to adulthood. In 1774, he drafted instructions for Virginia's delegation to the First Continental Congress, reminding King George III that he no longer ruled Virginia. Two years later, for the Second Continental Congress, Jefferson drafted the Declaration of Independence, proclaiming all men equal in inherent human rights and that government is the servant of the people.

Jefferson left Congress in 1776, returning to Virginia to collaborate with James Madison to end the Virginia state's religious establishment, resulting 10 years later in his Statute for Religious Freedom. He was elected and served as governor from 1779 to 1781, and afterward wrote *Notes on the State of Virginia,* recognizing the gross injustice of slavery, even though he diminished the natural abilities of Black people. In terms of religious freedom, he argued for a complete separation of church and state. As a member of the College of William and Mary Board, Jefferson effectively abolished their divinity school with the 1779 Jeffersonian Reorganization.

By the late 18th century, Jefferson began to sympathize with now-majority Protestant dissenters and religious movements that were challenging Virginia's dominant Church of England. Like the emigrated northern

Quakers who tolerated only their Protestant sect, various religious groups argued that they should become Virginia's state religion. Jefferson successfully countered that all would be better off equally free from state support and control.

Jefferson and James Madison's Virginia Statute for Religious Freedom, passed by the Virginia General Assembly on January 16, 1786, was a seminal document that kick-started a national effort to free religion from government interference and government from religious interference. That law became the basis for the First Amendment of the U.S. Constitution in 1791, prohibiting the Congress from establishing or limiting the free exercise of religion, later celebrated by Jefferson in 1802 as the "wall of separation between the church and state.

In 1784, Jefferson went to France after being named trade commissioner before then succeeding Benjamin Franklin as America's Minister to France. Returning in 1790 to become the first secretary of state, he vigorously opposed Alexander Hamilton's proposals for a more dominant central government. He lost the 1796 presidential election to John Adams, only to become his vice president. Four years later he defeated Adams to become our third U.S. president.

During his first term in 1803, Jefferson had the U.S purchase the Louisiana Territory and supported Lewis and Clark's westward explorations. He served a second presidential term and retired to Monticello for the last 17 years of his life. While there, at the age of 76, he organized, founded, and designed the University of Virginia, then served as its first leader. But he wasn't finished with his life's work.

Jefferson had lived his life so far in interesting, question-everything, innovative ways. He had read and been influenced by Francis Bacon's (1561-1626) scientific method requiring verification of all facts, even Bible facts. Isaac Newton (1642-1727), a Christian turned Unitarian, discovered and reported a naturally decaying/dissolving universe, making it possible for Jefferson and many other supporters of science and philosophy to become religious skeptics. Newton's scientific theories helped lead Jefferson to reject the conventional belief in the New Testament history of Jesus and the biblical story of divine worldly intervention. He did continue to believe in a prime mover, a creator of the universe, but one that was a non-interfering god.

Jefferson lived in a world of expanding opposition to church doctrines and dogmas, along with a growing rejection of state-church collaborations. He knew Christianity had joined with the powers of state as far back as the reign of Constantine in 350 C.E., when religion inexorably acquired new powers of enforcement backed by the Roman empire's might. Those who disavowed or disputed now-official Christian beliefs were deemed heretics and became targets of state-sanctioned violence. As such, apostasy was attempted by only the very brave or foolhardy.

Having studied law, Jefferson knew the Justinian Code of the Byzantine Emperor Justinian I (482–565), which gave all people natural rights, regardless of color or gender. Jefferson would also have seen Justinian's reign as the apogee of state/church authoritarian rule, reflecting the conviction dating back to Constantine that the unity of the Roman Empire presupposed unity of religious belief—for Justinian, orthodox Christianity. He had decreed the total destruction of paganism and persecuted non-Christians, even those with different Christian beliefs.

According to Karl Popper, Justinian's persecution of non-Christians, heretics, and philosophers in 529 planted the seeds for the Byzantine Dark Ages, culminating in the Catholic Church's Inquisition (1184 to early 19th century). Jefferson personally knew of the Spanish Inquisition's (1478 to 1834) brutal reign of terror to combat heresy and advance the Catholic and Spanish monarchy's autocratic power. In his lifetime, he saw state/church alliances gradually replaced by Enlightenment-informed beliefs in reason, religious tolerance, and individual liberty. Steven Pinker, in *Enlightenment Now*, said that Enlightenment thinkers insisted that we use reason to understand our world, and "not fall back on generators of delusion like faith, dogma, revelation, authority, charisma, mysticism, divination, visions, gut feelings, or…sacred texts."

By Jefferson's time, science and reason had opened the door just a crack to allow in the light of religious examination and inquiry. In an 1819 letter to William Short, he wrote admiringly of Epicurus, stating that the Greek philosopher's doctrines contained "everything rational in moral philosophy which Greece and Rome have left us." But he thought Plato dealt in mysticisms incomprehensible to the human mind; he hated Plato's idea of a soul that survived death. Jefferson nevertheless professed belief in a presumably *spiritual* Second Coming and judgement after death.

The Scientific Revolution began well before Jefferson's time in the mid-16th century with Copernicus's cosmology, lasting up to about the time of his proclaimed heroes, Sir Francis Bacon (1561-1626) and Isaac Newton

(1643-1727). The Age of Enlightenment begins then with another of his heroes, John Locke (1632-1704). Jefferson called Bacon, Locke, and Newton "the three greatest men that have ever lived, without any exception."

To understand why Jefferson looked up to those men is to better understand Jefferson. For one, Sir Francis Bacon led in establishing the British colonies in North America, especially Jefferson's native Virginia. Bacon believed, as did Jefferson later, that the world is best understood using "inquiry, knowledge, and belief of truth." As for Newton, his scientific discoveries, namely his formulation of the laws of motion and universal gravitation, led his contemporaries and then Jefferson to embrace science over mysticism.

Jewish philosopher Spinoza (1632-1677) didn't make Jefferson's top three list, but he influenced Locke and clearly influenced Jefferson's appeal to the "laws of nature and of nature's God." This was Spinoza's universalist religion, and like the later Deists, he believed in God but not that God ever changed the order of nature. Locke's and Jefferson's libraries both contained Spinoza's collected works, which maintain that ethical truths are discovered through human reason.

Locke, advocating for religious tolerance in his *Letters Concerning Toleration*, claimed that the state could not enforce a state religion without creating social disorder. He and Jefferson agreed that reason and tolerance govern human nature; Locke, unlike Jefferson, continued to believe in revelation and an inspired Bible.

Jefferson acknowledged fellow Deist Hermann Samuel Reimarus (1694-1768), the father of the quest of the historical Jesus. Reimarus argued that biblical miracles including Jesus's resurrection could be naturally explained, saying that the evangelists invented predictions of the resurrection. He identified Jesus as a mortal, apocalyptic Jewish prophet and pointed out the differences between what he said and what the apostles said. For Reimarus, Christianity was based on fabrication.

The gospel writers and early Christians adopted Jewish scriptures because, except possibly for Luke, they were Jewish and expected the coming of the Messiah. The Jewish Jesus, long before Christianity was a thing, preached in the temple to other Jews, warning them to repent and be ready for the second coming. To transform Jesus into a god, early disciples and eventually the gospel writers worked backward to fit to the Old Testament prophecies and transformed the man Jesus into the divine Christ. Neither Jefferson nor Reimarus believed in the Old Testament God or the divinity of Jesus. Jefferson did seem to believe in a deist-type God and in justice administered in an afterlife but perhaps not in a heaven or hell.

Tutored and educated by ministers, Jefferson grew up with the Bible and began life as an Anglican. But, per Charlotte Allen, author of *The Human Christ*, "his philosophical readings led him to espouse natural religion over organized Christianity while still in his twenties." And she notes that his "Nature's God" in the Declaration of Independence is the God of English Deism.

Over time, Jefferson settled upon the deistic belief in a non-interfering God. He adopted clergyman and political theorist Joseph Priestley's Unitarian belief that one could accept Jesus's teachings without believing that he was God.

Jefferson wrote in 1773 that he had read Priestley's *Corruptions of Christianity* and *Early Opinions of Jesus* "over and over again; and I rest on them...as the basis of my own faith." Jefferson could find no explicit New Testament claim that Jesus was God, and identified verses in which divinity was denied, such as Mark 10:18: "Why do you call me good? No one is good but God alone."

As vice president between 1798 and 1799, Jefferson often discussed religion with Benjamin Rush, a prominent Philadelphia doctor and respected scientist and Universalist (an all-will-be-saved Christian), and he promised Rush that he'd write down their shared religious views. In September 1800 as a presidential candidate being attacked as an infidel, Jefferson renewed his promise to Rush, intending to write his views so as to politically displease neither the rational Christian nor Deist.

Good and bad, weak, and strong—like most humans, Jefferson deserves praise and criticism. In a book about the Bible and religion, it's fair game to question his motives, morals, and means. Jefferson grew up with family slaves, inherited, owned, and, by age 21, managed them in a slave-dependent society. He objected to slavery in principle but not in personal practice. Jefferson lived large, earned small, and became obsessed with building and rebuilding Monticello and furnishing it in fine fashion. He ultimately became a captive to his lifestyle and discovered it could be maintained only with the labor of slaves.

Consider that Thomas Jefferson was born into colonial society where slavery had been taken for granted for more than 100 years and, by 1750, close to half of his native Virginia's population were slaves. Protected by law, slavery existed in all 13 American colonies in 1776. Slaveholders included most of the signers of the Declaration of Independence and almost half of the Constitutional Convention delegates. Of the other founding fathers, George Washington and James Madison owned slaves; even Benjamin Franklin owned a few. Nevertheless, these men and most of the founders and delegates believed slavery should be abolished—but only gradually. Their collective beliefs never resulted in national abolition legislation.

That he inherited slaves from both his father and his father-in-law, John Wayles, and that many others owned slaves is no defense. Some slaves learned low-level trades, and others learned farming or domestic skills—but they all remained slaves. Jefferson, as maybe the most intelligent and educated founding father, knew better, and yet not during his life nor in his will did he grant freedom to his slaves, excepting only a few of his offspring with his slave Sally Hemings.

George Washington and Benjamin Franklin did walk their talk and exited slave ownership. Washington freed his slaves in his 1799 will, and Franklin not only freed his but then became instrumental in abolitionist society. Jefferson, however, not only owned many slaves but also defended slaveholder rights. As a young man, he did advocate for the end of slavery and, of course, that all men are created equal. Over the years, though, he felt powerless to effect change while both forming and then preserving the Union. Fearing the end of the republic and a possible slave insurrection, he said, "we have the wolf by the ears, and we can neither hold him, nor safely let him go. Justice is in one scale, and self-preservation in the other."

Remember that, for most of his life, Jefferson was a politician—meaning that he needed to account for public opinion and to compromise to get anything done. To him, declarations, constitutions, and laws with social consequences "gore people's oxen" and required give and take to fairly allocate those burdens and hopefully some benefits. Ideally, personal and public ethics govern that process. Nobody faults "all men are created equal," but some complain that slaves weren't specifically included in the Declaration of Independence or the Constitution. The most salient reason I've heard for exclusion is that inclusion would have been a republic deal-killer, that Georgia and South Carolina would have then opted out. Jefferson, then ambassador to France, wasn't directly involved in that constitutional convention but long had advocated for eventual emancipation, which was the hope of the compromise that counted slaves as three-fifths of a person. Perversely, it didn't hasten emancipation and arguably set the stage for our Civil War.

Jefferson died on July 4, 1826, 50 years after the signing of the Declaration of Independence. Omitting nearly five decades of other extraordinary public services, he wrote only this epitaph:

> HERE WAS BURIED
>
> THOMAS JEFFERSON
>
> AUTHOR OF THE
>
> DECLARATION
>
> OF AMERICAN INDEPENDENCE
>
> OF THE
>
> STATUTE OF VIRGINIA
>
> FOR
>
> RELIGIOUS FREEDOM
>
> AND FATHER OF THE
>
> UNIVERSITY OF VIRGINIA
>
> BORN APRIL (13), 1743
>
> DIED JULY 4. 1826

Jefferson recognized that the principles he included in the Declaration of Independence hadn't been fully realized. He knew, too, that the essential-to-democracy separation of church and state was a battle that would be fought again and again. The success of both, he knew, would be vital to the survival of our free United States republic.

PART 3: JEFFERSON'S BIBLE

Jefferson, considered one of the most intelligent and educated of all the U.S. presidents, was a complicated man of his time. He was also ahead of those times. Well versed in philosophy and history, he developed strong negative views about religion and the Bible.

The New Testament Bible had its detractors and doubters long before Thomas Jefferson. (He didn't address the Old Testament.) Even Jesus's early and later disciples disagreed about who Jesus was, man or God, or both. Of the many early Bibles and writings advocating widely disparate religious approaches, only the four gospels and Paul's epistles were ultimately included in the 27 books that comprise the New Testament. Discussion and disagreements over what constituted the Jesus message were resolved and an early Bible became commonly accepted by Christian authorities and followers by the middle of the second century.

According to John Barton, editor in chief of the Oxford Research Encyclopedia of Religion, in his *A History of the Bible*, the first generation of what we call Christians were mostly illiterate and practiced their faith only according to oral traditions. Christianity wasn't even an official thing until the fourth century C.E. during the reign of Constantine. Before that time, Jesus's followers were a small, oppressed group, with a few members writing in an environment of persecution. Following the advent of an official Bible and, then, centuries of study, the text is still an enigma because its authors wrote creatively, informed by personal interests and biases. To many, those gospels weren't seen as inerrant and exact, but rather as stories and traditions about Jesus. After countless copies and transcriptions, there's no such thing as an authoritative New Testament, only variants of not even original and often criticized texts.

In *The Human Christ*, Charlotte Allen noted that contrary to the *gospel* truth, "the non-Christian ancient world was convinced that Jesus' father had been a mere mortal, that he was born in Nazareth...not in Bethlehem, that he had worked no miracles, and that his resurrection from the dead had been a matter of wishful thinking on the part of his disciples."

None of the progression of Bible history surprised William James, who in *The Varieties of Religious Experience* effectively summed up Jefferson's earlier ideas: "...history shows...religious geniuses (Jesus) attract disciples and produce groups of sympathizers. When these groups get strong enough to 'organize' themselves, they become ecclesiastical institutions with corporate ambitions of their own. The spirit of politics and the lust of dogmatic rule are then apt to enter and to contaminate the originally innocent thing..."

Controversy has always swirled around the Bible and the quest to discover the essence of its key character, Jesus. But before modern times, the power of the church, especially with state enforcement, meant that Jesus was who the church said he was. Jefferson, in an 1814 letter to N.G. Dufief, wrote that the Spanish constitution designated Roman Catholicism as the one and only, and as such always true, religion, and it prohibited the practice of any other. During the Inquisition, excommunication, social ostracism, and torture kept Bible criticism underground and to a minimum.

Not until more than a millennia after the first generally accepted Bible, in the wake of the changes brought on by Martin Luther and the Protestant Reformation, in addition to all that was made possible by the invention of the printing press, did society begin to overcome the tyranny of the entwinement of state and church.

The famous early Enlightenment Deist Thomas Chubb, in his 1741 *Discourse On Miracles*, just before Jefferson's birth, wrote of his disbelief in miracles and went on to dismiss Jesus's virgin birth and resurrection. He, like Jefferson later, maintained that Paul of Tarsus distorted Christianity from what Jesus believed and taught. Similarly, when Jefferson was still in his early 30s, Gotthold Ephraim Lessing published Hermann Reimarus' *Fragments*, a strictly human account of Jesus. About that same time, Presbyterian minister turned Unitarian Joseph Priestley began his search for the historical Jesus.

Jefferson had read Priestley's *An History of the Corruptions of Christianity* and *An History of Early Opinions Concerning Jesus Christ*, and the two men later met in Philadelphia in 1797 and became friends. They shared similar thoughts on religion and would compare the doctrines of ancient philosophers to those of Jesus. In April 1803, per encyclopediavirginia.org, Jefferson asked Priestley to write a precursor version of his ultimate *The Life and Morals of Jesus of Nazareth,* "omitting the question of Jesus' divinity and rendering the…character, and doctrines of Jesus…to the standard of reason, justice and philanthropy."

Jefferson had occasionally espoused Christian bromides, like telling a bereaved spouse that he/she might meet their departed in the afterlife, mostly as a means of ameliorating harsh political criticism that he was an infidel. He avoided expressing his true views, publicly insisting that religion was between a man and his God. Privately, though, Jefferson wrote to Benjamin Rush in 1803 reaffirming his Christianity and support for Jesus, ascribing to Jesus "every *human* excellence." With this letter to Rush, he included a copy of his April 9, 1803, letter inviting Joseph Priestley to write the religious views that Jefferson had earlier promised Rush that he'd write. As a third-year president with no free time, he still managed to outline his major gospel revisions. Priestley could not fulfill Jefferson's request, though, having become severely ill by 1800 and dying in February 1804.

Jefferson's initial goal was to produce a digest of Jesus's moral doctrines extracted from "…his [Jesus's] own words from the Evangelists," which he first did in March 1804 in a few nights in Washington, D.C., and titled it *The Philosophy of Jesus of Nazareth*. Using two copies of the *King James Version Bible*, Jefferson clipped out New Testament verses, pasted them onto 46 pages of a blank book, and had it bound. In that now lost first draft, Jefferson distilled from gospels "the very words only of Jesus," which he described "as distinguishable as diamonds in a dunghill." Soon after Jefferson finished this version, "…too hastily done…the work of one or two evenings…," he considered a revision, which he didn't get to for 15 years.

As a student of biblical history, Jefferson knew the Jewish Jesus expected no spiritual afterlife, but rather preached repentance to prepare for an imminent restoration of God's kingdom on earth. Jesus, like his predecessor John the Baptist and other contemporary Jews and Jesus's disciples, expected a second coming of God, who would pass judgment on both the living and resurrected dead. Those not worthy would cease to exist and the worthy would be rewarded with an Eden-like eternal earthly life.

Jefferson, pursuing accurate scriptures, wisely discounted zealot Paul's distortions of Jesus's message. Further, he recognized Matthew, Mark, Luke, and John as biased in favor of an early organization and establishment of an institutional church. Jefferson nevertheless accepted much gospel hearsay. He fudged on the hereafter and only deleted obvious evangelical miracles and myths.

Jefferson recognized that after orthodox Jews rejected Jesus's message, and following Paul's proselytizing spin, non-Jewish Christians came to believe judgement would be only spiritual. That is, on souls without bodies: Heaven above for the saved and hell below for the unrepentant and disbelievers. Gospel writers, especially the so-called Luke and John, subscribed to this view that became standard Christian belief and tacitly accepted by Jefferson, at least in public.

Jefferson, eight years out of politics, claimed to be his own (Christian) sect, and in an 1816 letter to Francis Adrian Van der Kemp called Jesus the "first of human sages," that his philosophy "is far superior" because Jesus preached "universal philanthropy, not only to kindred and friends, to neighbors and countrymen, but to all mankind." Jefferson believed in God, but he rejected the notion of Jesus's divinity and of the not-gospel-supported Trinity. As a "firm theist," he rejected biblical miracles and Jesus's resurrection.

As a gifted writer, innovator, and political influencer, it should be no surprise that in Jefferson's later years he personally took on his long-held goal of advancing the historical human Jesus and his gems of morality by redacting and effectively editing the traditional Christian Bible.

Jefferson blamed the Bible's mistaken elevation of Jesus to God status initially on Plato, who he thought wrote fantasy, then on Paul, who set the false spiritual stage, and finally on evangelists, who wrote the biblical script leading to a centuries-long distorted Christianity. Plato had advanced the concept of *souls* originating from the stars and returning after death. As a Greek Jew, Paul, even before the term Christianity existed, turned kingdom-on-earth Jesus from human prophet and sage into the *mystical* founder of a kingdom-in-heaven religion. Mark, Matthew, Luke, and John reported and enhanced Paul's imagined Jesus as *divine*, which was then accepted and adopted by developing institutional Christianity through to Jefferson's time and still today.

By age 76, Thomas Jefferson had vanquished official and oppressive state religion in Virginia and in the Declaration of Independence referred to the Laws of Nature and of Nature's God rather than to the God of Christian and Jew. He had influenced the Constitution and the Bill of Rights but had one last battle to fight. Self-serving biblical distortions of his admired Jesus's teachings had long stuck in his craw. Even if he needed to razor-cut and destroy multiple expensive copies of the new *King James Version Bible* and glue those preferred passage clippings into a new book, he felt compelled to set the biblical story straight.

In 1819 and into 1820, Jefferson resumed his 1804 task, again cutting out excerpts from the *King James Version Bible,* this time from six New Testament volumes, two each of a Greek/Latin, an English, and a French version. These clipped passages he glued in chronological order into a single volume, which he had bound in book form. He omitted references to Jesus's miracles and his resurrection, as well as passages that he believed were later embellishments. Jefferson sought to clarify and highlight Jesus's moral teachings, which, earlier to John Adams, he said were "the most sublime and benevolent code of morals which has ever been offered to man."

So, between 1819 and 1820, he wrote *The Life and Morals of Jesus of Nazareth,* now the subject of this, *Jefferson's Bible.* With this last written work, he reinforced his and our country's commitment to the separation of church and state. Jefferson knew from history that our republic would not likely survive unless we could squelch the inevitable attempts to reestablish state/church autocratic control.

Was it arrogant of Jefferson to rewrite the hallowed Bible for his personal use? Yes, maybe like his arrogance to draft the Declaration of Independence and to write the Virginia Statute for Religious Freedom.

Lori Anne Ferrell, historian author of *The Bible and the People,* says almost everybody edits the Bible. "Even people who read the Bible regularly only read parts of it. People read selectively. They read the parts they believe or the parts that give them comfort. For most people, the Bible is a cut-and-paste job. It's just that Jefferson actually takes a scissors or a knife and actually excises the parts he doesn't think should be in there."

Jefferson wrote in the embryonic days of historical and textual biblical scholarship—before two ensuing centuries of successful attempts to distinguish the historical Jesus from the lord of the Apostles' Creed, the mythical Jesus who became God and was God's only son. With my layman, non-theological, non-credentialed, yet science-oriented approach, I echo Jefferson with commentary and critiques that he might make today of his originally selected Bible passages.

Some say Jefferson should have made his true beliefs public. But consider that Anglican and Christian denominations then believed in a literal or at least inerrant Bible, and among literate whites they were virtually the only shows in town. Had Jefferson expressed his deep discontent with the widely revered Bible, he would not been able to attend the College of William and Mary, serve in the Virginia legislature, or been invited to draft the Declaration of Independence. So, he waited until late in life to, again *privately,* edit out the distortions that he found in the ubiquitous, publicly treasured *King James Version Bible*.

Jefferson claimed that his Bible was personal and private, but, as with all his meticulously preserved letters, he likely intended to influence future generations. He didn't preserve his earlier "hastily done" version, yet he failed to destroy his red leather-bound and professionally printed *The Life and Morals of Jesus of Nazareth*. That redacted and edited cut-and-paste single-edition, which Jefferson bequeathed and passed down to generations through his daughter and granddaughter, would finally be purchased by the Smithsonian Institution in 1895 from great-granddaughter Carolina Randolph.

Since the "atheist" or "infidel" label was then the political kiss of death, Jefferson called this Bible his own private version, perhaps fearing for his reputation and legacy, or perhaps he thought that the time for his Bible ideas was premature. But survive it did, and clearly this is the time to revisit and reevaluate *The Jefferson Bible*.

* * *

Debate continues among religious scholars about the meaning of Jefferson's choices of passages that he included in his Bible. Many subsequent editions of *The Jefferson Bible* contain introductions "proving" that Jefferson held the evangelical, Unitarian, or agnostic religious views of the publisher or editor. Often their purpose has been to promulgate editors' already held theological biases and beliefs.

This *Jefferson's Bible* merely speculates with comments how Jefferson might have updated his cut-and-paste project if he knew today's Bible history and facts. If he felt totally freed from the political and reputational restraints of publicly editing and redacting the traditional Bible, his "senior thesis" might accept and incorporate my and others' current comments and those facts learned since his death.

This presentation of Jefferson's complete original work and my and others' commentary assumes no need for a religious affiliation or for any prior Bible study or familiarity. Regular Bible readers will recognize some favorite familiar passages and perhaps some less familiar ones. Jefferson selected those passages that represented for him enduring and universal values parallel to his "all men are created equal"-espousing Declaration of Independence.

In 2021, after two centuries of immigration from around the world resulting in a more diverse religious environment, fewer Americans believe that the Bible is literally true. About half in a recent Gallup poll believed that the Bible is the inspired word of God, but not everything in it should be taken literally, and 30 percent called the Bible an ancient book of fables and history.

Belief in the traditional Bible, however, still matters in U.S. politics. George W. Bush and, especially, Donald Trump relied on Evangelical Christian voters, 40 percent of the American population, to get elected. Amoral, money-grubbing, dishonest, hypocritical, indicted Trump disturbingly waved a prop Bible, expressed newfound support for the Evangelical anti-abortion movement, got elected in 2016, appointed three religious Supreme Court judges, and is re-running in 2024.

So, how would Jefferson as a politician fare today—say, as a candidate for president in the 2024 election? He might not be accused of being a heretic or atheist, but he would probably still have to keep his unorthodox beliefs and ideas to himself for fear of alienating voters.

Jefferson thought multi-denominational Christianity and even pluralism was beneficial to democracy and "most friendly to liberty, science, & the freest expression of the human mind," but he was premature in predicting that Christianity would eventually be replaced in the U.S. by a more enlightened form of religion that rejected Jesus's divinity and belief in miracles.

As Jefferson expected, the United States is becoming more secular. However, Christianity is overrepresented in the U.S. Congress. According to a January 2013 Pew poll, since 2007, the share of the U.S. Christian population dropped from 78 to 63 percent. And yet, Christians make up 88 percent of the voting members of the 118th Congress sworn in on January 3, 2023 (with six percent identifying as Jewish, just under four percent identifying as "don't know/refused," and the remainder consisting of Muslims, Hindus, Buddhists, and others).

So, as Christianity declines, what fills the void in society and the body politic? Could it be a clearer idea of the value and limitations of the Bible and a move toward motivation by a Spinozan, enlightened self-interest rather than traditional scripture? Do we need a reminder of the importance of how Jefferson's religious beliefs played a foundational role in his abiding commitment to religious freedom and the separation of church and state? Yes, and yes.

There's an increasing trend that asks if we should value good art by a bad artist. Well, we might also ask if we should value religious advice from an imperfect, slave-owning, independence-declaring man like Thomas Jefferson. I say, yes.

As a product of his volatile and changing political and state/religious times, this prone-to-action man finally decided to put his now-famous pen to the universally accepted Christian Bible.

Part 4: The Jefferson Bible and Comments

What follows is *The Jefferson Bible,* along with comments reflecting what the scholarly Christian world has learned about the historical Jesus in the nearly 200 years since Thomas Jefferson completed his imperfect original.

The primary gospel writers' abbreviations are Mark - Mk., Matthew - Mt., Luke - Lk., John - J., Thomas -T., and Sayings gospel - Q., followed by chapter and verse(s) references true to Jefferson's original. I've then added duplicate or similar gospel—chapter and verse—passage references not in his original. New Testament is N.T., and Old Testament/Hebrew Scripture is O.T.

Jefferson's complete original passages are in *italics* followed by my comments in bold. I retain duplicate passages in the Jefferson original with only minor biblical passage edits and language updates.

The Life and Morals of Jesus of Nazareth- Redux

Jefferson began with the birth of Jesus minus most myths and miracles:

And it came to pass in those days, that there went out a decree from Caesar Augustus, that all the world should be taxed, ... And all went to be taxed, everyone into his own city. And Joseph also went up from Galilee, out of the city of Nazareth into Judaea to the city of David, called Bethlehem (because he was of the house and lineage of David) to be taxed with Mary his espoused wife, being great with child. And so it was, that, while they were there, the days were accomplished that she should be delivered. And she brought forth her first born son, and wrapped him in swaddling clothes, and laid him in a manger, because there was no room for them in the inn. And when eight days were accomplished for the circumcising of the child, his name was called Jesus." (Lk. 2:1-7, 21) And when they had performed all things according to the law of the Lord, they returned to Galilee, to their own city Nazareth. And the child grew, and waxed strong in spirit, filled with wisdom: And when he was twelve years old, they went up to Jerusalem, after the custom of the feast. And when they had fulfilled the days, as they returned, the child Jesus tarried behind in Jerusalem: and Joseph and his mother knew not of it. But they, supposing him to have been in the company, went a day's journey; and sought him among their kinfolk and acquaintances. And when they didn't find him, they turned back again to Jerusalem, seeking him. and it came to pass, that after three days they found him in the temple, sitting in the midst of the doctors, both hearing them and asking them questions. And all that heard him were astonished at his understanding and answers. And when they saw him, they were amazed: and his mother said to him, son, why have you dealt with us this way? Your father and I have sought you with sorrow. And he went down with them, and came to Nazareth, and was subject to them: And Jesus increased in wisdom and stature. (Lk. 2:39, 40, 42-48, 51, 52)

Jefferson did not believe in Jesus's virgin birth as a miracle fulfillment of Hebrew scripture prophesy. As an accomplished *King James Version* bible student, he would have known that those prophecies expected the messiah to be human—not divine. Nevertheless, he needed a beginning Bible storyline, and so he led off with Luke's storytelling of Jesus's birth in Bethlehem. December 25th? It's a date picked around the winter solstice, long celebrated by Egyptians (Ra) and pagans (Yule). In the 4th century C.E., church leaders, needing to compete, drew on the Roman festival of Saturnalia and transposed those festivities onto

the date of December 25, marking the birth of Jesus and a new holiday.

Scholars agree that Jesus likely was born in the year 4 B.C.E. but don't know where he was born. Probably it was Nazareth, since Bethlehem would have been a miracle 145 km, 31-hour walk for the about-to-deliver Mary. Also, the no-room-at-the-inn passage isn't supported by Paul's letters or by Mark's earlier gospel, so it's likely a myth. Rounding out Jesus's unknown youth story is Luke's telling of 12-year-old Jesus's super-theology performance in the temple.

Mary, the Bible-named mother of Jesus, is mostly a mystery, as is his father, Joseph. Jesus may have been Mary's first-born child, but other Bible passages describe him having (perhaps older) brothers and sisters. Jefferson, of course, left out the virgin birth, shepherds keeping watch, troops of the heavenly army (angels), generations of genealogies, and a traveling star leading the astrologers from the east. These were common literary devices of the time to show the importance of a king or emperor's birth, like for Caesar and Buddha.

Mark, the first Bible writer 30 years after Jesus's death, doesn't mention Jesus's birth, suggesting it wasn't known or not thought of as significant. Matthew and Luke used Mark as a source, each creating their own birth narrative. Jefferson kept Luke's miracle of 12-year-old Jesus's astounding elders in the temple but left out Matthew's prophecy-fulfilling escape trip to Egypt and John's turning of water into wine.

In fact, we know nothing about Jesus's birth, childhood, or young adulthood before Mark's account of his baptism by John the Baptist—the historic beginning of Jesus's public life around age 30. These birth stories were intended to set the stage for the arrival of an important holy man who sought to introduce a life-enhancing concept of loving your neighbor and even your enemies.

Now in the fifteenth year of the reign of Tiberius Caesar, Pontius Pilate was the governor of Judaea, and Herod was the tetrarch of Galilee.... (Lk. 3:1-2) John did baptize in the wilderness, (Mk. 1:4) And this same John had clothing of camel's hair, and a leather girdle about his loins: and he ate locusts and wild honey. People came to him from Jerusalem, all of Judaea, and all the region around Jordan, and were baptized by him in the Jordan River. (Mt. 3:4-6) Jesus came from Galilee to Jordan to John to be baptized by him. (Mt. 3:13) And Jesus was about 30 Years of age. (Lk. 3:23) After this he went to Capernaum, he, and his mother and his brethren (brothers), and his disciples: and they continued there not many days. And the Jews' Passover was at hand, and

Jesus went to Jerusalem, and found in the temple those that sold oxen, sheep, and doves, and changers of money. And when he had made a scourge of small cords, he drove them and the sheep and oxen all out of the temple: and poured out the changers money and overthrew the tables; and said to those who sold doves, take these things out; do not make my Father's house a house of merchandise. Afterwards, Jesus and his disciples traveled to Judaea: and he stayed with them and baptized. (J. 2:12-16; 3:22) Now when Jesus had heard that John was cast into prison, he departed into Galilee; (Mt. 4:12) For Herod himself had sent for and laid hold upon John, bound him in prison for Herodias' sake, his brother Philip's wife: for he had married her. For John had said to Herod, it is not lawful for you to have your brother's wife. Therefore, Herodias had a quarrel against him and would have killed him, but she could not: for Herod feared John, knowing that he was a just and holy man, and he observed him and heard him gladly. ...On his birthday Herod made a supper for his lords, high captains, and chief estates of Galilee. When the daughter of Herodias came in and danced and pleased Herod and his guests, the king said to the damsel, ask of me whatever you want, and I swear I will give it to you... up to half of my kingdom. The daughter asked her mother, what shall I ask for? and she said the Head of John the Baptist. ...Straightaway she returned to the king and said, I wish that you will give me, on a platter, the head of John the Baptist. And the king was exceedingly sorry; yet for his oath's sake and for that of his company, he would not reject her. Immediately the king sent an executioner and commanded his head be brought and he went and beheaded him in prison; and brought his head on a platter and gave it to the damsel: and the damsel gave it to her mother. (Mk. 6:17-28) And Jesus and his disciples returned to Capernaum; and right away on the sabbath he entered the temple and taught. And they were astonished at his doctrine: for he taught them as one who had authority, and not as the scribes. (Mk. 1:21-22; also Mt. 14:1-14)

Jesus was a contemporary of a historic and well-known itinerant preacher, John the Baptist, one of countless Holy Land messiahs, preachers, and prophets. John baptized his many followers, including Jesus, in the Jordan River. John reputedly claimed the end of times was near and all must repent, and a greater prophet or messiah would follow him. Jesus did follow and some think he continued John's apocalyptic message mostly unchanged, though others think he deemphasized it. The Jesus Seminar considers Jesus's message more about the present, citing his major parables of the Good Samaritan, the Prodigal Son, the Great Banquet, and others.

Jefferson excluded the Jordan baptism in which God shouts from the sky, as well as Jesus being tested by the devil in the desert, and stuck to the probable facts of Jesus's age, travels, and

practical teachings as he cut and pasted snippets mostly from Mark but also from Matthew, Luke, and John. They all built the case that John the Baptist was a great prophet who told of a yet greater man to come, namely Jesus.

Following John's imprisonment and murder by Herod Antipas, Jesus returned to Galilee, which was being ruthlessly controlled by the Romans, continued where John left off, and began his short (one-to-three year) public life. Mark, especially, relayed the early-Christian community sentiment of the eminence of Jesus as an extraordinary prophet of the many in his day.

Jefferson's next entry about Jesus and his disciples concerns a practical, present-day solution to hunger.

At that time Jesus on the Sabbath day went through a cornfield and his disciples were hungry and began to pluck the ears of corn and to eat. But when the Pharisees saw it, they said to him, behold your disciples do that which is not lawful to do on the sabbath day. But Jesus said to them, have you not read what David did when he and those who were with him were hungry: how he entered into the house of God and ate the consecrated bread, which was not lawful for him or his disciples to eat but only for the priest? Or have you not read in the law how that on the sabbath day the priests in the temple profane the sabbath and are held blameless? And when he departed, he went to their synagogue and behold there was a man with a withered hand and they asked him, is it lawful to heal on the sabbath day? for they hoped to accuse him. And he asked them, what men here among you who has one sheep that falls in a pit on the sabbath day, will not lay hold on it and lift it out? How much better then is a man than a sheep? Wherefor it is lawful to do well on the Sabbath day. (Mt. 12:1-5, 9-12) And he said to them, the sabbath was made for man and not man for the sabbath. (Mk. 2:27) Then the Pharisees went out, and held a council against him, how they might destroy him. But when Jesus knew of it, he left that area and great multitudes followed him. (Mt. 12:14-15; also Mk. 2:23-28 and Lk. 6:1-5)

Capernaum is a town on the northern edge of the Israel Sea of Galilee and likely where itinerant Jesus often stayed and preached, perhaps in synagogues or at the local homes of disciples. Jesus and his apostles were generally thought to be illiterate and wrote nothing, but perhaps Jesus could read Hebrew (and maybe Greek), which might explain his knowledge of the Hebrew scriptures and why "they were astonished at his doctrine: for he taught...as one that had authority."

The point here is that Jesus was a serious teacher and knew his Jewish scripture. He

critically questioned religious authorities, and especially their legalistic orientation, like dietary and laws of Sabbath activities, and the hypocritical practices of the Pharisees and scribes, who then took offense and wanted to silence him.

Jefferson, who helped inspire the U.S. Revolutionary War and was an observer of the lead up to the French Revolution, must have appreciated and identified with the revolutionary nature of Jesus. The lesson is that human religious and government institutions tend to be self-serving, and as such diminish individual freedoms. As a result, they need to be ever revitalized by courageous actors like Jesus and, later, Jefferson.

And it came to pass in those days that he went up onto a mountain to pray and continued all night in prayer to God. And when it was day, he called his disciples to him: and of them he chose twelve, whom he named apostles; Simon (whom he also named Peter), and Andrew his brother, James and John, Philip and Bartholomew, Matthew and Thomas, James the son of Alpheus, and Simon called Zealotes, and Judas the brother of James, and Judas Iscariot, who also was the traitor. And he came down with them, and stood in the plain, and in the company of his disciples, and a great multitude of people out of all Judea and Jerusalem, and from the seacoast of Tyre and

Sidon, who came to hear him. (Lk. 6:12-17; also Mk. 3:13-19 and Mt. 10:1-4)

Twelve close disciples came to be called Jesus's apostles, but his family of followers may have numbered 25 or more. However, the number 12 likely symbolized the 12 tribes of Israel; the Jewish gospel writers suggested that Jesus was the promised Messiah who heralded the new Jewish religious order. The names of the apostles as listed by Luke differs somewhat from the apostles named in the other gospels (discrepancies likely recognized by Jefferson), and little is known about their real identities. Only Jesus's brother James is later *historically* identified, around 100 C.E., by Jewish historian Josephus.

What is the primary element of leadership? Followers, of course, and the point here is that Jesus attracted devoted, often poor, and destitute followers, showing that his message filled a need and had taken root already during the first century C.E.

And seeing the multitudes, he went up to a mountain: and when he was set, his disciples came to him; and he taught them saying: Blessed are the poor in spirit: for theirs is the kingdom of heaven. Blessed are they that mourn for they shall be comforted. Blessed are the meek: for they shall inherit the earth. Blessed are they who hunger and thirst after righteousness: for they shall be filled. Blessed are the merciful: for they shall obtain mercy. Blessed are the pure in heart: for they shall see God. Blessed are the peacemakers: for they shall be called the children of God. Blessed are they who are persecuted for righteousness' sake: for theirs is the kingdom of heaven. Blessed are you when men shall revile you, and persecute you, and say all manner of evil against you falsely, for my sake. Rejoice, and be exceedingly glad: for great is your reward in heaven; for so persecuted were the prophets before you. (Mt. 5:1-12) But woe to you who are rich! for you have received your consolation. Woe to you who are full, for you shall hunger; who to you who laugh now, for you shall mourn and weep; woe to you when all men shall speak well of you, for so did their fathers to the false prophets. (Lk. 6:24-26)

These are Matthew's Beatitudes (inspired by Hebrew Bible psalms) from the Sermon on the Mount. Luke had similar Beatitudes from the Sermon on the Plain. The Bhagavad Gita and the traditional writings of Buddhism predate the Bible and some of those far earlier "humility and absence of ego teachings" resemble the Beatitudes but with different wording. Gospel evangelists clearly relied both on earlier writings and current conventional wisdom to create their chapters. Jefferson included similar gospel passages by different evangelists and,

regardless of their source, they remain classic advice on how to live a virtuous life.

You are the salt of the Earth: but if the salt has lost its savor, where shall it be used? it is thenceforth good for nothing, but to be cast out and trodden under foot of men. You are the light of the world. A city that is set on a hill cannot be hid. Neither do men light a candle, and put it under a bushel, but on a candle stick; and it gives light to all who are in the house. Let your light so shine before men, that they may see your good works, and glorify your Father in heaven. Think not that I have come to destroy the law or the prophets, I have come not to destroy but to fulfill. For I say to you, until heaven and earth pass, one iota or part shall in no wise pass from the law, until all be fulfilled. Whosoever therefore shall break one of these least commandments, and shall teach men so, he shall be called the least in the kingdom of heaven: but whosoever shall do and teach them, the same shall be called great in the kingdom of heaven. For unless your righteousness exceeds the righteousness of the scribes and Pharisees, you shall in no case enter into the kingdom of heaven. You have heard said by them of old time, that you should not kill, and whosoever shall kill shall be in danger of the judgement. But I say that whoever is angry with his brother without a cause shall be in danger of judgement.... Therefore, if you bring your gift before the altar, and there remember that your brother has a complaint against you; leave there your gift before the altar and go, first to be reconciled to your brother, and then come back and offer your gift. (Mt. 5:13-24; also Q., Mk., and T.)

This well-known "salt of the earth" parable exhorts us to set a personal good example with both our charitable actions and good deeds. Matthew talks of the kingdom of heaven, but Jesus primarily offers practical, common-sense advice on reconciliation and forgiveness in this life. Disciples, first be a good example and let your light shine before all men. First deal justly with your brother, then bring your gift to the altar.

Agree with your adversary quickly while you are with him, lest at any time the adversary deliver you to the judge and the judge deliver you to the officer and you be cast into prison, you shall no means come out then until you have paid your whole debt. You have heard it said by them of old time, that you should not commit adultery: but I say to you that whosoever looks upon a woman with lust has committed adultery with her already in his heart. And if your right eye offends you, pluck it out and cast it away: for it is better for you that one of your members should perish, than your whole body should be cast into hell. And if your right hand offends you cut it off and cast it away, for it is better for you that one of your members should perish, than your whole body should be cast into hell. It has been said whosoever shall put away his wife, let him give her a writing of divorcement: but whoever puts away his wife, saving for the cause of fornication, causes her to commit adultery: and whoever shall marry her that is divorced also commits adultery. Again, you have heard it has been said in old times you shall not swear an oath but shall perform to the Lord your oaths: but I say do not swear at all, neither by heaven, for it is God's throne: nor by earth, for it is his footstool: neither by Jerusalem, for it is the city of the great King. Neither shall you swear by your head because you cannot make one hair white or black. But let your communication be yay, yay; nay, nay; for whatsoever is more than these come of evil. (Mt. 5:25-37; also Mk. 9:43-48)

Jesus often criticized the hypocrisy of the establishment Pharisees, who ignored their offenses against others as they made their ostentatious spiritual offerings. We're encouraged here to make peace with our fellow humans before making a show of our devotion. Jesus warns disciples not to tolerate sin, especially adultery.

Like all public servants, Jefferson was criticized by self-serving politicians without "clean hands" and could relate to the evils of biblical self-serving Pharisees. The lesson is that being kind and at peace with your brother and sister,

meaning everybody, is more important than any show of public charity or devotion.

For Luke, Mark, and Paul, divorce is prohibited, but Matthew allows an exception for infidelity, indicating ambiguity among early Christians about Jesus's teachings. Not an issue for Jefferson and his one wife, Martha Wayles, with whom he had six children. She died in 1782 and Jefferson never remarried. However, the bit about lust being adultery may have given Jefferson more than a moment's pause.

You have heard that it has been said, an eye for an eye and a tooth for a tooth: but I say you should resist not evil: but whosoever shall smite you on the right cheek, turn to him the other also. And if any man will sue you at the law, and take away your coat, let him have your cloak also. And whosoever shall compel you to go a mile, go with him. Give to him who asks you, and from him who would borrow of you, don't turn him away. You have heard that you should love your neighbor and hate your enemy. But I say, love your enemies, bless those who curse you, do good to they who hate you, and pray for them who spitefully use you, and persecute you. That you may be children of your heavenly Father: for he makes his sun rise on the evil and on the good and sends rain on the just and the unjust. For if you love those who love you, what is your reward? Don't the publicans (tax collectors) do the same? And if you love only your brethren, what do you do more than others? Do not even the publicans do so? and if you respect only your brethren, what do you do more than others? don't even the publicans do this? (Mt. 5:38-47) And if you lend to those whom you hope to receive, what thanks do you have? For sinners also lend to sinners, to receive as much again. But love your enemies, and do good, and lend, hoping for nothing back; and your reward shall be great, and you shall be the children of the Highest: for he is kind to the unthankful and to the evil. Be you therefore merciful, as your Father also is merciful. (Lk. 6:34-36; also, source Q.?)

These passages mark the fundamental shift from the law of the Tanakh, or Hebrew Bible, to the characteristic approach of Jesus, and likely these are close to his actual words. This "love your enemies" passage reflects the essential Jesus by countering the age-old, nearly universal human inclination to strike back if hit or to resist if forced to do something.

Jefferson acknowledged here how the Hebrew Bible's lessons of equivalent justice and retribution for wrongdoing changed with Jesus's message of love and forgiveness for every fellow human. I suspect that Jefferson neither borrowed nor lent zero interest to good or poor credit risks and may not have loved his political enemies but that he appreciated this idea of generosity of spirit.

Take heed that you do not give alms to be seen by others, otherwise you'll have no reward from your heavenly Father. When you give alms do not sound a trumpet before you, as the hypocrites do in the synagogues and in the streets, that they may have glory of men. I say to you, they have their reward. But when you give alms let not your left hand know what your right hand does: that your alms may be in secret: and your Father who sees you in secret shall reward you openly. And when you pray, you shall not be as the hypocrites: who love to pray standing in the synagogues and in the corners of the street, that they may be seen by men. I say to you, they have their reward. But when you pray enter your closet and when you have shut the door, pray to your Father in secret; and your Father who sees in secret shall reward you openly. But when you pray, don't use vain repetitions as the heathen do: for they think that they shall be heard for their long prayers. Be rather not like them for your Father knows what things you have need of before you ask him. (Mt. 6:1-8)

This is a sharp rebuke of and a characteristic criticism of the scribes', Pharisees', and temple leaders' ostentatious practice of the letter, but not of the spirit of the Jewish law. Mathew's words for Jesus here counsel us to be true to ourselves and to our principles—to keep our devotion between us and our God.

Certainly, Jefferson in his day witnessed fellow politicians wearing their goodness and religious devotion on their sleeves, but he knew their true characters when they were outside of public view. Jefferson insisted that religion for him was private—between a man and his God.

After this manner pray: Our Father which art in heaven. Hallowed be thy name. Thy Kingdom come. Thy will be done on earth as it is in heaven. Give us this day our daily bread. And forgive us our debts, as we forgive our debtors. And lead us not into temptation but deliver us from evil: For thine is the kingdom, and the power, and the glory, forever, Amen. For if you forgive men their trespasses, your heavenly Father will also forgive you: But if you don't forgive men their trespasses, neither will your Father forgive your trespasses. Moreover, when you fast, be not as the hypocrites, of a sad countenance: for they disfigure their faces, that they may appear to fast. I say to you that they have their reward. But when you fast, anoint your head and wash your face; that you appear to men not to fast, but just to your Father in secret: and your Father who sees in secret, shall reward you openly. (Mt. 6:9-18; also, Lk. 11:1-4)

Matthew's version of the Our Father is the Christian world's most accepted prayer, and, if he prayed, it's one that Jefferson would have recited privately.

Lay not up for yourselves treasures upon earth, where moth and rust do corrupt and where thieves break through and steal: but lay up for yourselves treasures in heaven where neither moths nor rust do corrupt and where thieves do not break through nor steal your treasure; there also will your heart be. The light of the body is the eye: if therefore your eye be honest, your whole body shall be full of light. But if your eye is evil your whole body shall be full of darkness. If therefore the light that is in you is darkness, how great is that darkness! (Mt. 6:19-23)

Itinerant Jesus, universally pictured in simple garb wearing sandals, eschewed the material possessions of this world to focus on his and our spiritual wellbeing.

This was perhaps more of an aspiration of Jefferson's since he owned slaves and was well-off in his public and private life. Nevertheless, Jefferson appreciated Jesus's reminder that the important elements in life are spiritual, like acts of kindness, and unlike the accumulation of material wealth.

No man can serve two masters: for either he will hate the one and love the other; or else he will hold to the one and despise the other. You cannot serve God and mammon. Therefore, I say to you, take no thought for your life, what you eat, or what you drink; nor yet for your body, what you shall put on. Isn't life more than meat, and the body more than fine clothes? Behold the birds of the air: for these don't sow, nor do they reap, nor gather into barns; yet your heavenly father feeds them. Are you not much better than they? Which of you by thinking can add a foot to his stature? And why think about fine clothing? Consider the lilies of the Field, how they grow; they don't toil, neither do they spin: and yet I say to you, that even Solomon in all his glory was not dressed like one of these. Wherefore, if God shall clothe the grass of the field, which today is, and tomorrow is cast onto the oven, shall he not much more clothe you? Oh, you of little faith. And therefore, take no thought saying, what shall we eat? Or what shall we drink? Or wherewithal shall we be clothed? (For all these things do the Gentiles seek:) for your heavenly Father knows that you need all these things. But seek first the kingdom of God, and his righteousness; and all these things shall be provided to you. Take therefore no thought for tomorrow: for tomorrow shall take thought for the things by itself.... (Mt. 6:24-34; also, Lk. 12:22-30)

You cannot be a slave to both God and your bank account—an expected theme coupled with modern words—is an idea that was likely contemplated and preached by Jesus, who always favored the poor over the rich.

Matthew's famous Lilies of the Field parable to his Jewish audience advises not to fret the small stuff—and that it's *all* small stuff except for the honoring of God. This passage also encourages us to appreciate nature, its beauty, resilience, and independence from human direction or cultivation or care.

Jefferson may have admired the idea of having God's nature provide for his earthly needs but surely was preoccupied with day-to-day existence negotiating revolution and freedom from the British crown. He practiced taking care of his own material needs, as he somewhat successfully served God and mammon.

Judge not, that you be not judged. For with what judgment you judge, you shall be judged... (Mt. 7:1-2) Give, and it shall be given to you: good measure, pressed down, shaken together, and running over, shall men give back to you. (Lk. 6:38) And why do you notice the spec in your brother's eye but consider not the beam in your own eye? Or how will you say to your brother let me pull out the spec of your eye and behold a beam is in your own eye? You hypocrite, first cast out the beam in your eye and then shall you see clearly to cast out the spec in your brother's eye. Give not that which is holy unto the dogs, neither cast your pearls before the swine, lest they trample them under their feet, and turn again and rend you. (Mt. 7:3-6; also Lk., T., and Q.)

Don't criticize and judge, just as you do not want to be judged. Per Matthew, Jesus is cautioning us that it is easier to find fault in others than uncovering and first dealing with our own shortcomings. Jesus repeatedly criticized the Jewish religious leaders, the Pharisees, and scribes for finding fault in everyone but ignoring their own much greater faults. Matthew has Jesus use dogs and pigs to represent those who reject his message and suggests that disciples just move on.

It's easy to imagine Jefferson reacting to having been judged by fault-laden opposing politicians and activists of his time. Faced with opposition to his innovative political and religious ideas must sometimes have felt like he had been casting pearls before swine.

Ask, and it will be given to you; seek and you will find; knock, and it will be opened for you: for everyone who asks receives; and he who seeks finds; and to he who knocks it will be opened. Or what man is there whom if his son asks for bread will give him a stone? Or if he asks for a fish, will give him a snake? If you then, being evil know how to give good gifts to your children, how much more shall your Father, who is in heaven, give good things to them who ask him? Therefore, all things that men should do to you, do you even to them: for this is the law and the prophets. (Mt. 7:7-12; also Lk., T., and Q.)

Matthew tells us that Jesus preached for us to be generous, and not only to our family and friends. This is a variation of the universal religious adage known as the Golden Rule— "Do unto others as you would have them do unto you"—or, as Jesus's contemporary, Rabbi Hillel, said, "What you hate, don't do to another."

Some have questioned the possible severe discipline enacted by his overseers, but Jefferson reportedly personally treated and housed his slaves well—though he wasn't so kind as to free them all, only the 10 to whom he was closely related. He apparently had youthful ideals about freedom for all men, but politically settled for stating the principle in the Declaration of Independence and hoping for the future possibility of the abolition of slavery.

Enter at the straight gate: for the gate is wide and the way is broad that leads to destruction: and many will go in that way. Because straight is the gate and narrow is the way that leads to life, few will find it. Beware of false prophets, which come to you in sheep's clothing but inwardly they are ravening wolves. You will know them by their fruits. Do men gather grapes from a thorn bush or figs from a thistle? A good tree grows good fruit, but a corrupt tree grows evil fruit: a good tree cannot grow evil fruit, nor can a corrupt tree grow good fruit. Every tree not growing good fruit is cut down and burned. Wherefore by their fruits you will know them. (Mt. 7:13-20; also Lk., T., and Q.)

The "straight gate" represents the smooth and easy way leading to destruction, but the approach to life and virtue is narrow and more difficult.

Surely, Jefferson saw in his political life, as we see in politics today, many wolves in sheep's clothing, and he recognized evil men from whom no good would ever come. He observed that, universally, the fruits of our acts, not what we proclaim, are the best measure of who we really are.

A good man out of his good treasure of heart brings forth good things: and an evil man out of his evil treasure brings forth evil things. ...every idle word that men speak; they shall give an account of in the day of judgment. For by your words, you will be justified and by your words you will be condemned. (Mt. 12:35-37) Therefore, whoever hears these sayings of mine and act on them will be like a wise man who built his house upon a rock: and the rains came, and the floods came, and the winds blew, and beat upon that house, and it did not fall, for it was founded upon a rock. And for everyone who hears these sayings of mine and doesn't act on them, will be like a foolish man who built his house on sand: and the rains came, and the floods came, and the winds blew, and beat upon on that house, and it fell, and great was its fall. And when it came to pass when Jesus had ended these sayings the people were astonished at his doctrine, for he taught as one having authority and not as the scribes. (Mt. 7:24-29; also Lk. and Q.)

Matthew has Jesus, like the many prophets and seers of his day, warn us to beware of those pretending to be good but who are evil. The fate of every person who hears and does not obey the words of Christ builds on sand and will fall on God's judgment day.

Jefferson built his own character on the rock of study, reason, and of continuous self-improvement. With some training as an architect, he could appreciate the analogy of foolishly building on a poor foundation. Jefferson wasn't an adherent of the great fall but expressed belief in some sort of judgement after death. Not especially focused on the afterlife, he prioritized acting in daily life.

When Jesus came down from the mountain, great multitudes followed him. (Mt. 8:1) And he went around about the villages teaching. (Mk. 6:6) Come to me all of you who labor and who are burdened, and I will give you rest. Take my yoke and learn from me; for I am meek and lowly in heart: and you will find rest in your souls. For my yoke is easy and my burden is light. (Mt. 11:28-30; also, Lk. and Q.)

Leaving out the miracles, Jefferson cut and pasted snippets from the gospels of Matthew and Mark describing how Jesus touched a prevalent need among the poor and dispossessed, as he preached through humility rather than self-aggrandizement and self-promotion.

No one would mistake Jefferson for the meek or lowly, and he bore a heavy political burden, but he apparently appreciated the sentiment.

A Pharisee asked Jesus if he would eat with him. Jesus went to the Pharisees house and sat down to eat. And a woman in the city who was a sinner when she knew that Jesus set to eat in the Pharisees house, she brought an alabaster box of ointment. And she stood at his feet behind him weeping and began to wash his feet with tears and wiped them with the hairs of her head and kissed his feet and anointed them with the ointment. When the Pharisee who invited him saw this, he said to himself, if this man were a prophet, he would have known that this woman who touched him is a sinner. And Jesus answering him said, Simon I have something to say to you: there was a certain creditor who had two debtors: the one owed 500 pence and the other 50. And when they had nothing to pay, he forgave them both. Tell me then which of the debtors will love him most? Simon answered and said I suppose that he to whom he forgave the most. And he said to Simon you have judged right, and he turned to the woman and said to Simon see this woman? I entered your house you gave me no water for my feet, but she washed my feet with tears and wiped them with the hairs of her head. You didn't give me a kiss but this woman since the time I came in has not cease to kiss my feet. You didn't anoint my head with oil, but this woman anointed my feet with ointment. (Lk. 7:36-46; also, Mk., Mt., and J.)

Luke had Jesus renew his regular critique of the Pharisees, yet he ate a meal with one. Jesus criticized his host's judgmental attitude and preached a lesson of acceptance of repentant sinners. Jefferson cut Luke's last lines (Lk. 7:47-50) where the man Jesus forgave the woman's sins.

Jefferson experienced much more criticism than forgiveness in his political life and could agree with this lesson in fairness and civil treatment: that the Pharisees weren't above other men. Jefferson, in principle at least, was a champion of the common man—the individual, the farmer—and is perhaps known best for the phrase "all men are created equal."

Jesus' brethren came, stood outside, and called for him. A large group sat around him and told him that his mother and brothers asked for him. Jesus answered them saying, who is my mother or my brother? And he looked at those who sat around him and said, behold you are my mother and my brother. Whomever shall do the will of God, that person is my brother and my sister and my mother. (Mk. 3:31-35; also, Mt., Lk., and T.)

Jesus, shown here by Mark as not close, perhaps in conflict with his immediate family, nonetheless expressed that all the world is his and our family. His message is to love everyone, not just our immediate biological family and personal friends.

Unfortunately, when Jefferson died in deep debt, his family sold 130 slaves, virtually all the members of every slave family from Monticello, to pay his creditors. His will did free five more (of 10 total), all Hemings family members.

In the meantime, an innumerable multitude gathered, and Jesus first said to his disciples, beware of the influence of the Pharisees which is hypocrisy. For there is nothing covered that shall not be revealed; neither hid, that shall not be known. Whatever you have spoken in darkness shall be heard in the light; and that which you have spoken in the ear in closets shall be proclaimed upon the housetops. And I say to you my friends be not afraid of they who killed the body and after that have no more that they can do. But I will forewarn you whom you shall fear: fear him who after he killed has power to cast into hell: I say do fear him.... (Lk. 12:1-5; also, Mt. and Q.)

Secret evils will eventually be known. Especially you should fear those who can do you spiritual harm. Through Luke here, Jesus warned his disciples to expect to be physically persecuted for spreading his warnings of the approaching judgment day and his preaching of the need to repent.

Jefferson certainly knew of secret political plots and persecutions by French and British royalty and clergy. He seems to have accepted at least the possibility of the revelation of all secrets in the form of judgment after death.

Are not five sparrows sold for two farthings and not one of them is forgotten before God? But even the very hairs on your head are all numbered. Fear not because you have more value than many sparrows. And one of the company said to him, Master, speak to my brother that he divides the inheritance with me. And he replied, Man, who made me a judge or a divider over you? (Lk. 12:6-7, 13-14)

Luke has Jesus tell us that God watches over all equally, and that we're created equal in value. He had Jesus decline involvement in a financial squabble.

Jefferson famously saw the worth of each individual and their right to a free existence— other than his and all slaves everywhere who he thought might eventually be freed but then exported to Africa. Jefferson feared rapid emancipation would threaten the Union.

...And he said to the crowd: Take heed and beware of covetousness: for a man's life consists not of the abundance of things which he possesses. Jesus spoke of a certain man who had become rich farming his land. The man thought, what shall I do, because I have no room to store my fruits? So, he said I will pull down my barns and build bigger ones; and there I will store my fruits and my goods. And I will say to my soul that you've laid up goods and supplies for many years—take your ease, eat, drink, and be merry. But God said to him, you fool, this night your soul will be required of you: then for whom will those stored goods benefit? So, he is one who stores up treasure for himself but is not rich towards God. (Lk. 12:15-21; also T.)

Luke's Jesus here preaches that life's important values are spiritual—not material. In the end, death will come as a thief in the night for all of

us and our physical possessions will do us no good.

Like the parable's rich farmer, Jefferson created an "abundance of things" building and ever expanding his Monticello plantation. Nevertheless, he did achieve a spiritual treasure as a statesman, succeeding in forming a free (eventually for all) republic.

And he said to his disciples...Take no thought for your life, what you shall eat: neither for the body, what you shall put on. Life is more than meat and the body is more than clothing. Consider the ravens: for they neither sow nor reap and have neither storehouse nor barn; and God feds them: how much better are you than the birds. And which of you by thinking can add one inch to his stature? If you are not able to do that little thing, why do you think about the rest? Consider the lilies how they grow: they toil not, they spin not; and yet Solomon in all his glory was not arrayed like one of these. If God so clothed the grass, which is today in the field, and tomorrow is cast in the oven, how much more will he clothe you, O, you of little faith. And seek not what you shall eat, or what you shall drink, neither be of doubtful mind. For all these things do the nations of the world seek after: and your Father knows you have need of these things. But rather seek the kingdom of God and all these things will be given to you. Fear not little flock: for it is your

Father's good pleasure to give you the kingdom. Sell what you have and give alms; provide yourselves things which won't become old, a treasure in the heavens that won't fail, where no thief approaches nor moth corrupts. For where your treasure is, there will be your heart also. .... And look like men who wait for their lord, when he will return from the wedding; that when he comes and knocks, they will open for him immediately. Blessed are those servants whom the lord comes, he shall find watching; I say to you, that he shall prepare himself, and make them sit down to eat and will come and serve them. And if he shall come in the second watch, or in the third watch and find them so, blessed are those servants. And know that if the master of the house had known what hour the thief would come, he would have watched, and not suffered his house be broken in. Therefore, you be ready for the Son of Man who comes at an hour when you think not. Peter then asked, Lord do you speak this parable just to us or to everyone? And Jesus said, who then is that faithful and wise servant, whom his lord shall make ruler over his household, to give them their portion of meat in due season? Blessed is that servant, whom when his lord comes finds him faithful. Of a truth I say to you, that he will make him ruler over all that he has. But, if that servant says in his heart, my lord will be delayed, and then beat the men servants and maidens, and eats and drinks to be drunken; the lord of that servant will come in a day when he doesn't look for him, and in an hour when he is not aware, and will cut him asunder, and that servant, who knew his lord's will, and did not prepare himself, nor act according to his will, shall be beaten with many lashes. But he who didn't know his lord's will, but committed offenses, shall be beaten with only few lashes. For to whom much is given, much shall be required: and to whom men have committed much, of them they will ask more. (Lk. 12:22-48; also Mt., T., and Q.)

This is Luke's variation of Matthew's Lilies of the Fields parable, which tells us to trust God to provide for your needs as he does for fauna and flora. The gospels depict an itinerant Jesus who doesn't know when he will have his next meal or where he will sleep.

In contrast, Jefferson was born into a well-to-do plantation family and throughout his life provided for his own earthly needs often on credit. But he believed that nature's God provided for the natural environment, although not always with regular sun and rain for his plantation crops.

...And he said to the crowd: When you see a cloud rise out of the west, you say a shower is coming—and it does. And when the south wind blows you say there will be heat; and so, there is. You hypocrites! You can discern the face of the sky and the earth; but how can you not discern

this time? And why can you not discern what is right? When you go with your adversary to the magistrate... be careful that you may be delivered by him; lest he haul you before the judge, and the judge deliver you to the officer, and the officer cast you into prison; where you shall not depart until you have paid every last cent. (Lk. 12:54-59; also Mt., T., and Q.)

Don't you get what I'm saying? Luke reports what must have been a common knowledge of early Christian communities that Jesus's message was often misunderstood and ignored. It surely frustrated Jesus that his simple but unconventional message could be hard to understand and accept even among his disciples and followers.

Jefferson must have had similar thoughts when he encountered resistance to the colonies' political divorce from monarchy rule and transition to independent self-rule. His dedicated advocacy for the separation of church and state similarly triggered misunderstanding and disagreement.

Those present told Jesus of the Galileans Pilate had killed and then mingled their blood with their sacrifices. And Jesus asked, do you suppose that these Galileans were sinners more than other Galileans, because they suffered such things? No, I say: but unless you repent, you shall all likewise perish. Or those eighteen, upon whom the tower in Siloam fell and killed, do you think they were sinners above all men who lived in Jerusalem? I say no: but unless you repent, you will all perish likewise. (Lk. 13:1-5; also Mt. and T.)

Luke tells of Galileans who were killed by Pontius Pilate while they were offering sacrifices; they wanted Jesus to explain why bad things happened to good people who worship. They imagined this great tragedy signified great guilt. Jesus said that the victims weren't greater sinners and added that those killed by the falling of the tower of Siloam likewise weren't killed because of their sinfulness. He then repeated his message that the time for repentance was now.

Jefferson likely believed in sin and repentance, yet he understood that sin and natural forces weren't related.

.... Jesus also spoke this parable; a certain man had a fig tree planted in his vineyard; and he came seeking fruit from it and found none. Then he said to the caretaker of his vineyard, behold these three years I came seeking fruit of this fig tree and find none: cut it down; why does it encumber the ground? And the caretaker answered him, Lord, let it alone this year and I shall cultivate and fertilize it: and if it bears fruit,

well: and if not, then after that you should cut it down. (Lk. 13:6-9)

Jesus's recurrent lesson in this Luke passage was to eliminate the spiritually extraneous in your life and focus on the spiritually productive.

In his time, Jefferson was witness to the autocratic mentality of the church and the abuses of monarchial rule. He saw that French Revolution needed to "cut it down" and discard their unproductive system of governance. Jefferson personally saw that the existing power of the monarchy wouldn't be relinquished willingly or peacefully. As a revolutionary, Jefferson helped plant a new constitutional tree that we've seen bear the productive fruit of liberty.

A certain Pharisee sought to dine with Jesus, and he went in to eat. The Pharisee saw that Jesus did not (ritually) wash before dinner. And the Lord said to him, you Pharisees make clean the outside of the cup and platter; but your inward part is full of ravening and wickedness. You fools! did not He who made without also make that which is within? But if you give alms of what you have, behold, all things are clean to you. But woe to you Pharisees! for you tithe mint, rue, and all manner of herbs and ignore the judgement and love of God: the tithing you ought to have done, and not to leave the other undone. Woe to you

Pharisees! for you love the upper seats in the synagogues, and greetings in the markets. Woe to you, scribes and Pharisees, hypocrites! for you are as graves that don't appear, and the men who walk over them are not aware of them. One of the lawyers asked him, Master, are you also reproaching us? Jesus said, Woe also to you lawyers! for you load men with grievous burdens to bear, and you yourselves don't touch the burdens with a single finger. Woe to you, lawyers! for you have taken away the key of knowledge: you didn't enter yourselves, and you hindered those who were entering. And as he said these things to them, the scribes and Pharisees began to vehemently urge and provoke him to speak of many things: lying in wait for him and seeking to catch something he said that they might accuse him. (Lk. 11:37-54)

This is like Luke 7:36-46, with Jesus criticizing Jewish leaders displaying virtue on the outside but being corrupt within. Jesus's key motivation was to reform the abuses committed by the Jewish religious leaders of his day, not to found a complex, self-serving religion named after him.

Jefferson revered Jesus as a seer among seers, not as a god figure. As to the lawyer part, maybe Jefferson had a bad experience in commerce or government. Or is it possible that he remembered a little line from Shakespeare's *Henry VI*: "Let's kill all the lawyers"?

That same day Jesus went out of the house and sat by the seaside and great multitudes gathered towards him so that he went onto a ship and sat, and the crowd stood on the shore. He spoke many things to them in parables saying, behold a sower went forth to sow; and when he'd planted, some seeds fell by the wayside, and the birds came and devoured them; some seeds fell on stony ground where they had not much soil and they sprung up, but because the soil was not deep, when the sun was up, they were scorched, and because they had no roots they withered away; and some seeds fell among thorns, and the thorns sprung up and choked them; but other seeds fell onto good ground and brought forth fruit, some, one hundred-fold, some sixty-fold, some thirty-fold. Whoever has ears to hear, let him hear. (Mt. 13:1-9; also Mk., Lk., and T.)

This is Matthew's version of Jesus's aphorism that ends the Parable of the Wedding Feast: "many are called but few are chosen."

Jefferson sowed seeds of liberty, yet some of those seeds fell on the stony ground of those who had personally benefited from the monarchy and fought for its continued existence. We've seen recently in current times that some selfish, autocratic politicians aren't at all concerned about what benefits all. Rather,

their personal interests are the thorns that choke out the seeds of the common good.

Later, when Jesus was alone with his twelve apostles, they asked him about the parable. (Mk. 4:10) He said, ...When anyone hears the word of the kingdom and doesn't understand it, then comes the wicked one who steals away the good words which were heard in his heart: this is he who received the seed by the wayside; but he who received the seed in a stony place is the one who hears the word and received it with joy; yet the seed doesn't root in him but survives only for a while; until tribulation or persecution arises and by-and-by he is discouraged. He who received the seed among thorns is he who hears the word; but the cares of this world, and the deceit of riches choke the word, and he becomes unfruitful. But he who received the seed into the good ground is he who heard the word and understood it; that seed bears fruit, and brings forth some one hundred-fold, some sixty-fold, some thirty-fold. (Mt. 13:18-23; also Mk. and Lk.)

Matthew has Jesus offer this Parable of the Sower to his obviously dense apostles. This message about the "good word" of love and virtue can be heard and received or rejected in many ways.

Jefferson was materially well off and did value Jesus's sermons about love and forgiveness, not

toward just family but to all, and he realized the benefit to U.S. society. However, like everyone, he seemed to value some of Jesus's lessons more than others. He at least expressed hope that the "good fruits" of freedom would eventually benefit the slaves.

And he said to them, is a candle brought to be put under a bushel, or under a bed? and not to be set on a candlestick? For there is nothing hid, which shall not be exposed; neither was anything kept secret, but that it should come out. If a man has ears to hear, let him hear. (Mk. 4:21-23; also T., Lk., and Mt.)

Jefferson had multiple choices and picked Mark's passage, which, like Luke's, had Jesus tell his disciples that they had been given the light of goodness through his parables and that they should share it with all.

... The kingdom of heaven is like a man who sowed good seed in his field. But while men slept, his enemy came and sowed weed seeds among the wheat. When the wheat sprung up, so did the weeds. .... The man said to his servants: Let both grow together until the harvest; and then I will say to the reapers, gather first the weeds, bundle them to burn but gather the wheat into my barn. (Mt. 13:24-30; also T.) Then Jesus sent the

multitude away and went into the house: and his disciples came to him asking him to explain the parable of the weeds. He answered, the sower of good seed is the Son of Man; the field is the world; the good seeds are the children of the kingdom; but the weeds are the children of the wicked one; the enemy that sowed them is the devil; the harvest is the end of the world; and the reapers are the angels. As the weeds are gathered and burned in the fire, so shall it be at the end of this world. The Son of Man will send his angels and they shall gather out of his kingdom all things that offend and those who do iniquity; and will cast them into a furnace of fire; there shall be wailing and gnashing of teeth. Then shall the righteous shine forth as the sun in the kingdom of their Father. (Mt. 13:36-43)

Matthew has Jesus describe the later Christian community's fears of a hostile world—the weeds among their wheat—ending with a final judgement day.

It's unclear what Jefferson thought about hell and teeth-gnashing. He did seem to believe in a kind of justice or reckoning in the afterlife, maybe sans heaven's angels and hell's devils. This was perhaps an exception to his general dismissal of the supernatural.

Again, the kingdom of heaven is like a treasure hid in a field: which, when a man found it, he hid it and with joy went and sold all he had and bought that field. (Mt. 13:44) Again, the kingdom of heaven is like a merchant seeking goodly pearls: Who when he had found one pearl of great value, went, and sold all that he had and bought it. (Mt. 13:45-46; also T.)

Matthew has Jesus explain first the evil of deceit, then of investing all in a material treasure, implying the foolish attraction to temporal goods.

Jefferson invested in both material treasures like Monticello and spiritual good in the form of the new republic.

Again, the kingdom of heaven is like a net cast into the sea and gathered fish of every kind. When it was full, they drew near to shore, sat down, and gathered the good into vessels, but cast the bad away. So shall it be at the end of the world: the angels shall come and sever the wicked from the just and cast the wicked into the furnace of fire; there shall be weeping and gnashing of teeth. (Mt. 13:47-50) Jesus said to them, have you understood all these things? They answered, yes Lord. then Jesus said, therefore every scribe who is instructed to the kingdom of heaven is like a man who is a householder, who brings out of his treasure things new and old. (Mt. 13:51-52; also T.)

This is Matthew's version of good souls among the bad, many of whom are called but few are chosen.

Jefferson certainly believed in justice, but this passage is hard to reconcile with his disbelief of miraculous spirits who will sort the wicked from deserving souls at the end of time.

...So is the kingdom of God, as if a man should cast seed into the ground; and should sleep, and rise night and day, and the seed should spring up and grow, he doesn't know how. For the earth brings forth fruit of herself, first the blade, then the ear, after that the full ear of corn. But when the fruit is ripe, employs the sickle because the harvest has come. And... the Kingdom of God... is like a grain of mustard seed, which when it is sown in the earth is smaller than all the seeds....; but when it is sown, it grows up and becomes greater than all herbs and shoots out great branches; so that the birds of the air may lodge under its shadow. .... But he spoke to them only by parable; and when they were alone Jesus explained all things to his disciples. (Mk. 4:26-34; also T.)

Mark has Jesus explain his parables to his uneducated apostles. He has Jesus teach that small, dedicated actions such as his own message and his disciple's missionary future efforts can have a dramatic and growing effect.

Jefferson appreciated this message and knew the power of his and the founders' words and the leverage effects of those words growing into a declaration of freedom.

... a certain man said to him, Lord, I will follow you wherever you go. And Jesus said to him, foxes have holes, and birds of the air have nests: but the Son of Man has nowhere to lay his head. And he said to another, follow me. But that follower said, Lord, let me first to go and bury my father. Jesus said to him, Let the dead bury their dead: but you go and preach the kingdom of God. And another also said, Lord, I will follow you, but let me first go and bid farewell to those at my home. And Jesus said to him, no man having put his hand to the plough, and looking back, is fit for the kingdom of God. (Lk. 9:57-62; also Mt., T., and Q.) ... Jesus saw a publican, named Levi, sitting at the receipt of customs; and he said to him, follow me; And he left all, rose up, and followed him. And Levi made a great feast in his own house. (Lk. 5:27-29; also Mk. and Mt.)

Luke has Jesus say that he has no home, and that he's given up all material comforts and expects his followers to do the same. Perhaps, to Luke, Jesus's words mean that it's all or nothing in devotion to Jesus.

Certainly, Jefferson didn't subscribe to this approach in his religious practice. If anything, he

"looked back" to the care and management of his plantation. He always had a home.

Many publicans and sinners also sat together with Jesus and his disciples: for there were many and they followed him. And when the scribes and Pharisees saw him eat with these publicans and sinners, they said to his disciples how is it that he eats and drinks with publicans and sinners? When Jesus heard them, he said, those who are well don't need a physician, but rather it is those who are sick. I came not to call the righteous but to call the sinners to repentance. (Mk. 2:15-17; also Mt. and Lk.)

Jesus preached to sinners, toll collectors, prostitutes, and those he saw in need of spiritual health. Through Mark and all the evangelists, he disparaged the elitist social and religious scribes and Pharisees who considered themselves virtuous and above the sinners and publican common folk.

Jefferson, of course, wrote that not just the rich deserved rights but that human rights were God-given for all men. Common to his time and social circumstance, he didn't act on securing the rights of his slaves, but he did fervently hope for their eventual freedom.

Jesus spoke a parable: No man puts a piece of new garment onto an old: otherwise, the new makes a tear and doesn't match the old. And no man puts new wine into old bottles; else the new wine will burst the bottles and be spilled. New wine must be put in new bottles, and both are preserved. (Lk. 5:36-38; also T.)

Luke has Jesus quote probable common secular proverbs to draw a contrast between the old Judean and new Christian movements.

This practical common-sense advice probably appealed to Jefferson, who saw Jesus as an extraordinary secular sage—the best of his and maybe of all times.

And when Jesus had finished these parables, he departed. And when he came into his own country, he taught them in their synagogues, and they were astonished. They said how can this man be so wise and do such mighty works? Isn't this the carpenter's son? Isn't his mother called Mary and aren't his brothers James and Joses and Simon and Judas? And his sisters, aren't they all with us? How can this man know and teach all these things? Some listeners were offended. But Jesus said a prophet is without honor in his own country and in his own house. (Mt. 13:53-57; also Mk., Lk., J., and Th.)

Matthew shows a Jesus who is well versed in Jewish scriptures. He incidentally mentions the fact of Jesus's siblings, so Jesus wasn't an only child.

Jefferson, who could be considered a civic prophet, sometimes felt unappreciated in his own country and more honored when in France while serving as an ambassador. His fellow politicians undervalued his extraordinary level of learning and wisdom, and some belittled his unconventional federalist ideas. The parable above, minus the unincluded miracles at the end, likely struck a chord with him, maybe reminding him of those instances when he received little respect.

> ...when Jesus saw the crowds following him, he was moved with compassion because some had fainted from hunger, and they were scattered about like sheep without a shepherd. (Mt. 9:36) He called his 12 apostles to him and sent them forth two by two. (Mk. 6:7) He commanded them, don't go the way of the Gentiles and not into any city of the Samaritans; but rather go to the lost sheep of the house of Israel. Carry neither gold, nor silver nor brass in your purses, nor scrip for your journey, neither two coats, shoes, nor staffs: for the workman is worthy of his meats. And into whatever city or town you shall enter, enquire who in it is worthy; and reside there until you leave. And when you come into a house, honor it.

And if your house is worthy, let your peace come upon it: but if it is not worthy, let your peace return to you. And whosoever will not receive you or hear you, leave that house or city and shake off the dust of your feet. I say it will be more tolerable for the land of Sodom and Gomorrah on the day of judgment than for that city. I send you as sheep amid wolves. Be wise as serpents and harmless as doves. But beware of men: for they will deliver you up to the councils, and they will scourge you in their synagogues and you will be brought before governors and kings for my sake, for a testimony against them and the Gentiles. But when they persecute you in any city, flee into another: Fear them not therefore: for there is nothing covered. that shall not be revealed; and hid that shall not be known. What I tell you in darkness, you speak in the light: and what you hear preach from the housetops. And don't fear those who kill the body but are not able to kill the soul: but rather fear he who is able to destroy both soul and body in hell. Are not two sparrows sold for a farthing? And one of them shall not fall on the ground without your Father. But the very hairs on your head are all numbered. Fear you not therefore, you are of more value than many sparrows. (Mt. 10:5, 6, 9-18, 23, 26-31) And they went out and preached that men should repent. And the apostles gathered with Jesus and told him all things, both what they had done and what they had taught. (Mk. 6:12, 30)

Jefferson skips over the miracle of loaves and fishes that magically expanded to feed thousands. Here, instead, he focused on Mark and mostly Matthew's message of Jesus preparing and exhorting his disciples to spread the word and warning them to expect to encounter resistance, which he advised to ignore and move on to friendlier more receptive areas.

Jefferson would have been well aware of the political campaign principle, then and now: converting the enemy is unproductive: take care of your base voters/supporters and work to convince the undecided; and pay little heed to those firmly against you and move to more receptive areas.

After these things Jesus walked in Galilee: for he would not walk in Jewry, because the Jews sought to kill him. (J. 7:1) The Pharisees and certain of the scribes came to Jesus from Jerusalem, and when they saw some of his disciples eat bread with defiled (unwashed) hands, they found fault. The Pharisees and all Jews don't eat unless they wash their hands, holding to the tradition of their elders. And when they come from the market they don't eat unless they wash their hands. They hold many other rituals such as the washing of cups and pots and of brass vessels and tables. The Pharisees asked Jesus why his disciples did not follow the tradition of the elders and that they ate with unwashed hands? Jesus called all around and asked them to understand, he said, there is nothing from without a man that entering into him can defile him; but the things which come out of him, those can defile the man. And when he then entered the house, his disciples asked about the parable and Jesus said, can't you understand? Do you not perceive that whatever thing comes from without that enters a man cannot defile him; Because it entered not his heart but into his belly, and goes out into the drought, purging all meats? And he said that which comes out of the man, that defiles the man. For from within out of the heart of men can come evil thoughts, adulteries, fornications, murders, thefts, covetousness, wickedness, deceit, lasciviousness, an evil eye, blasphemy, pride, foolishness. All of these things come from within and defile the man. And from there Jesus arose and went to the borders of Tyre and Sidon, and entered into a house without telling anyone, but he could not hide. (Mk. 7:1-5, 14-24; also Mt. and Th.)

Germs and the benefits of hand washing were unknown in Jesus's time and still undiscovered when Mark wrote. The point here isn't hygiene, but rather that Jesus is again criticizing the established, legalistic purity rituals of the Jewish religious leaders. Mark has Jesus go on to list various sins and faults, leaving out an exorcism. The takeaway seems to be that what comes from the heart is more important than ritual.

Jefferson would have agreed with this list of sins and maybe added a few political offenses.

His disciples asked, who is the greatest in the kingdom of heaven? Jesus called over a little child and sat him in their midst and said, unless you are converted and become as little children, you will not enter the kingdom of heaven. Whomever shall humble himself as this little child is the greatest in the kingdom of heaven. (Mt. 18:1-4; also Mk., Lk., and Q.)

Matthew has Jesus preach the value of the simple humility of a child: Avoid the sophistry and intellectualization of the religious poohbahs and just respond to Jesus's simple message of love and forgiveness.

Jefferson described Jesus's ethical teachings as "primitive Christianity" before church leaders perverted it for their own status and power. Jefferson never took on a child's simple humility. Nevertheless, he abhorred the prideful, self-serving complication of Christianity over the ages.

Woe to the world because of offenses (sins)! For the offenses will come; but woe to that man by whom the offenses come! Wherefor if your hand and foot cause you to sin, cut them off and cast them from you: it is better for you to enter into life halt or maimed rather than have two hands or two feet to be cast into everlasting fire. And if your eye offends you pluck it out and cast it from you: it is better for you to enter into life with one eye, rather than having two eyes to be cast into hell fire. (Mt. 18:7-9) How do you think, if a man has a hundred sheep and one of them goes astray, does he not leave the ninety-nine and go into the mountains and seek the one which has gone astray? And if he finds it, I say to you, he rejoices more of that sheep than the ninety-nine which did not go astray. Even so it is not the will of your Father which is in heaven, that one of these little ones should perish. (Mt. 18:12-14) Moreover if your brother shall trespass against you, go and tell him his fault between you and him alone: if he will hear you, you have gained your brother. But if he will not hear you, then take with you one or two more, that in the mouth of two or three witnesses every word may be established. And if he shall neglect to hear them, tell it to the church: but if he neglects to hear the church, let him be to you as a heathen man and a publican. Then Peter came to him and said, Lord how often shall my brother sin against me, and I forgive him? Till seven times? Jesus said to him, I will not say to you not seven times, but rather until seventy times seven. (Mt. 18:15-17, 21-22) The kingdom of heaven is like a certain king who would take an account of his servants. And when he had begun to reckon, one was brought to him who owed him ten-thousand talents. But since he had no way to pay, his lord commanded him to be sold, and his wife, and children and all that he had, and payment to be made. The servant then fell down and worshipped him, saying, lord have patience with me, and I will pay you all. Then the lord of that servant was moved with compassion and freed him and forgave the debt. But that same servant went out and found one of his fellow servants who owed him a hundred pence: and he laid hands on him, and took him by the throat saying, pay me what you owe me. And his fellow servant fell down at his feet and begged him saying, have patience with me and I will pay you all. And he would not: but went and cast him into prison until he should pay the debt. So, when his fellow servants saw what he had done they were very sorry and came and told their lord what he had done. Then the lord called him said to him, oh you wicked servant, I forgave you all that debt because you asked me: should you not have also had compassion on your fellow servant, even as I had pity on you? And his lord was angry and delivered him to tormentors, until he should pay all that was due him. So likewise, shall my heavenly Father do also to you, if you from your hearts forgive not everyone his brother their trespasses. (Mt. 18:23-35; also Mk., Lk., Th., and Q.)

Matthew inserts here an extensive collection of Jesus's parables about the hellish consequences of failing to avoid temptation and sin. He has Jesus tell of the importance of forgiveness and of the failure to forgive.

Regarding compassion and forgiveness, Jefferson (per monticello.org) never personally beat a slave but did order their physical punishment through his overseers. Quasi compassionate?

After these things the Lord appointed seventy disciples and sent them two and two... to every city and place where he would go.... and said to them, the harvest is truly great, but the laborers are few.... Go your ways: behold, I send you forth as lambs among wolves. Carry neither purse, nor money, nor shoes: and salute no man on the way. And into whosoever house you enter, first say, Peace be to this house. .... And in the same house remain, eating and drinking what is served.... And into whatever city you enter... eat what is set before you. But whatever city you enter, if you are not well received, go on your way.... (Lk. 10:1-12; like Mt. 10:5, 6, 9-18, 23, 26-31)

This is a summarization of Luke's version of Jesus's command to spread the word of the kingdom of man.

Jefferson, not active in organized religion beyond his youth, wouldn't have supported these early disciples' missionary efforts. He didn't even approve public dissemination of his own version of Jesus's wisdom, now *The Jefferson Bible*. **He avoided its publication before his death but did bequeath his single**

leather-bound copy to his daughter, apparently intending it for posterity.

Now the Jews' feast of the Tabernacle was at hand. Jesus' brethren said to him, depart and go to Judaea so your disciples there may see your good works. For there is no man that does anything in secret, and he himself seeks to be known openly. If you do these things, you will show yourself to the world. For neither did his brethren believe in him. Then Jesus told them, my time is not yet come, but your time is now ready. The world cannot hate you, but it hates me, because I testify to its evil works. To his disciples he said, go to the feast but I will not, my time is not yet fully come. Jesus' abode was still in Galilee. But, when his brethren were gone, he also went to the feast, just not openly—in secret. Then the Jews sought him at the feast asking, where is he? And about him there was much murmuring by the people: some said he was a good man, others said nay—he deceives the people. But no man spoke openly of him for fear of the Jews. (J. 7:2-13) Now about the middle of the feast Jesus went to the temple and taught. And the Jews marveled saying, how does this unlettered man know to teach—having never learned? Jesus answered them, did not Moses give you the law, and yet none of you keep the law? Why do you go about to kill me? The people answered, you have a devil that plans to kill you. Jesus answered them, I have done one work and you all marvel. Moses gave you the rite of circumcision and on the sabbath you circumcise a man. If a man is circumcised on the sabbath so the law of Moses is not broken: are you angry at me because I have made man whole on the sabbath? Judge by righteousness, not appearances. Then some of them from Jerusalem asked, is this not he whom they seek to kill? But he speaks boldly, and they say nothing to him. Do the rulers know indeed that this is the very Christ? (J. 7:14-16, 19-26; also Mk., Mt., and Lk.)

The fourth evangelist John wrote in the late first century or early second century. He painted a world of darkness and disbelief, indicated that Jesus thought his time was not yet right, and foreshadowed Jesus's persecution and trial as the son of God. John advocates, here and throughout his gospel, for Jesus's divinity by calling him Christ (Greek for Messiah). Preacher-*man* Jesus objected to the current abuses of the Jewish Pharisees, their phony rituals, and false doctrines, and accordingly became a threat to their power and influence.

Much like Judaism in Jesus's time, governments in colonial America, as in Europe, closely adhered to a designated religion, with minorities persecuted for their beliefs. Jefferson helped lead a movement to end such practices and specifically struggled to legislate freedom from Virginia's state Anglican religion. His advocating for disestablishment earned him many opponents—competing politicians who

sought to diminish or eliminate him as a threat to their favored religious ideas.

The Pharisees heard the people murmuring such things concerning Jesus and the Pharisees and the chief priest sent officers to take him. But there was division among the people about him. Some would have taken him, and some would not: no man laid a hand on Jesus. Then the officers returned to the chief priests and Pharisees who asked, why have you not brought him? The officers answered, never has a man spoken like this man. The Pharisees replied, have you also been deceived? Have the rulers or the Pharisees believed him? His disciples don't know the law and are cursed. Nicodemus, a secret disciple (and/or a Pharisee), appealed to them, does our law judge any man before he has a hearing and knowing what he does? They answered, are you also from Galilee? Search and look to the scriptures: for no prophet is to arise out of Galilee. The group dispersed to their own homes. (J. 7:32, 43-53)

John says that the Pharisees, sensing a growing threat, attempt to discredit and arrest Jesus but discover his popular support even among their henchmen. Rather than deal with the issues that Jesus raises, they follow the standard political playbook of disparaging Jesus and circling the wagons of their dogma and customs.

They accuse this troublemaker of heresy and of disturbing the established religious order.

As a revolutionary against the British crown, Jefferson empathized with the gospel writers' depiction of the plight of Jesus. Jefferson's early years were as a subject to the British crown and in later years he was surely seen as a traitor to the crown.

Jesus went to Mount Olive and early the next morning returned to the temple, and the crowds gathered once more. He sat down and taught them. The scribes and Pharisees then brought him a woman taken in adultery; they placed her in the middle and said to Jesus, master, this woman was taken in adultery in the very act. Now Moses in the law commanded us that she should be stoned, but what do you say? They tempted him so that they might have reason to accuse him. Jesus stooped down and with his finger wrote on the ground as if he had not heard them. When they continued asking him, he stood up and said to them, he who is without sin among you, let him cast the first stone at her. And again, he stooped down and wrote on the ground and those who saw what he wrote, being convicted by their own conscience, left one by one beginning with the eldest even to the last. Soon Jesus was left alone with the woman standing nearby. When Jesus stood up and saw only the woman, he said to her, woman, where are your accusers? Has no man condemned you? She said, no man, Lord. And Jesus said to her, neither do I condemn you. Go and sin no more. (J. 8:1-11 only)

Here, John has Jesus double down against Pharisee eye-for-eye legalism and hypocrisy, and he reaffirmed the virtue of forgiveness. This well-known lesson in compassion remains valid. However, this parable wasn't included in John's earliest known gospel manuscript and scholars since Jefferson's time attribute it to a scribe or source other than John.

Ironically, Jefferson also knew of his opponents' faults and probably enumerated them, though not written in the ground but in his political campaign pamphlets. Those political enemies, in turn, didn't hesitate to cast the first stone at him.

And as Jesus passed by, he saw a man who had been blind from birth. His disciples asked him, master, who sinned, this man or his parents, that he was born blind? Jesus answered, neither this man nor his parents have sinned, but the works of God should be made manifest in him. (J. 9:1-3)

I say to you, he that enters not by the door into the sheep pen but climbs up another way is a thief and robber. He who enters through the gate is the shepherd. The porter opens the gate, the sheep hear his voice, he calls them by name and leads them out. He goes before them and they follow, for they know his voice. The sheep will flee from a stranger for they will not know his voice. (J. 10:1-5) John has Jesus speak a parable: I am the good shepherd: the good shepherd will give his life for the sheep. But a hireling who is not the shepherd sees the wolf coming, leaves the sheep and flees and the wolf catches and scatters the sheep. The hireling flees because he is a hireling and doesn't care for the sheep. I am the good shepherd and know my sheep and I am known by mine. And other sheep I have which were not of this fold: them also I must bring, and they shall hear my voice; and there shall be one fold and one Shepherd. (J. 10:11-16 only)

John here has Jesus first disabuse the then-common notion that a birth defect or physical abnormality must be related to a sin of the parents or the victim. He then famously describes Jesus's care and guidance of his human flock as the Good Shepard.

Jefferson focused on the common good of his fledgling nation and the importance and value of the individual. It's unlikely that he subscribed to this analogy of citizens as sheep led by a monarch-type shepherd or of unquestioning religious adherents led by an absolute pope-type leader.

As Jesus preached, a certain Lawyer stood up and tempted him saying, Master, what shall I do to inherit eternal life? Jesus said to him, what is written in the law? How do you read it? And the lawyer answered, you shall love the Lord your God with all your heart and soul and strength, and with all your mind; and your neighbor as yourself. Jesus said to him, you have answered correctly: do this and you shall live. But to justify himself, the lawyer asked Jesus, and who is my neighbor? Jesus answered, a certain man traveled from Jerusalem to Jericho, and fell among thieves who stripped him of his clothing, wounded him, and departed leaving him half dead. And by chance a certain priest came that way: and when he saw the victim he passed on the other side of the road. And likewise, a Levite came by the same place, looked at him and passed on the other side. But a certain Samaritan, as he journeyed, came where the man was and when he saw him, he had compassion for him. He went to him and bound up his wounds, pouring on oil and wine, and set him on his own beast and brought him to an inn and took care of him. The next morning before he departed, he took out two pence, gave them to the host and told him to take care of the man and whatever you spend more than this, when I come back, I will repay you. Which now of these three do you think was neighbor to him who fell among the thieves? And the lawyer said, he who showed mercy on him. Then Jesus said to him, go and you do the same. (Lk. 10:25-37 only)

This was an apparently well-known and characteristic Jesus' parable of the early Christian movement. Luke tells Jesus's story of the ostensibly holy and caring Jewish religious role models who didn't walk their talk—who preached compassion but didn't practice it in their daily lives by stopping to help others. Yet, an ordinary good Samaritan, from a then-disfavored Jewish sect, *did* show compassion and kindness to a social outcast in need.

A lawyer and public figure, Jefferson surely appreciated political talk, and he no doubt understood how campaign promises made by political candidates didn't always turn into policy once those candidates were elected to office.

And Jesus prayed, when he finished, one of his disciples said to him, Lord, teach us to pray, as John the Baptist taught his disciples. Jesus said, when you pray say, Our Father which art in heaven, Hollowed be thy name. Thy kingdom come. Thy will be done, as in heaven, so in earth. Give us by day our daily bread. And forgive us our sins: for we also forgive everyone that is indebted to us. And lead us not into temptation; but deliver us from evil. (Lk. 11:1-4; like Mt. 6:9-18) And he said to them which of you shall have a friend and go to him at midnight and say to him, friend lend me three loaves for a friend of mine on his journey has come to me and I have nothing to set before him? And he from within will answer and say, trouble me not: the door is now shut, and my children are with me in bed, I cannot rise and give them to you. Yet, because he is his friend and because of his importunity he will rise and give him as many loaves as needed. Ask and it shall be given to you; seek, and you will find; knock and the door will open. For everyone who asks receives; and he seeks finds; and to him that knocks, it will be opened. (Lk. 11:5-10) If a son asks bread of any of you that is a father, will you give him a stone? or if he asks for a fish, give him a snake? Or if he asks for an egg, give him a scorpion? If you then, being human, know how to give gifts to your children: how much more shall your heavenly Father give the Holy Spirit to them that ask him? (Lk. 11:11-13; also Mt., Th., and Q.)

This is Luke's version of Jesus's Our Father prayer and one of his most quoted lines, urging generosity even when it may be an effort.

It's been reported that Jefferson owned as many as 600 slaves over his lifetime, perhaps 130 at a time at Monticello. While not justifying his slave ownership, apparently his slaves were well housed, fed, and not treated harshly by him personally. However, at his direction and common to his plantation owner society, his overseers took care of hands-on corrective measures. Publicly, Jefferson said slavery was a hideous blot and a moral depravity, yet while he was alive, and only to honor a bargain, he freed two son slaves and allowed three others to

escape. And in his will, he freed five others, including two more of his and his slave Sally Hemings's children. So, was he being human in knowing how to give gifts to his children?

Jesus went to the house of one of the chief Pharisees to eat bread on the sabbath and they watched him. And there was a man before him who had dropsy. Jesus asked the lawyers and Pharisees, is it lawful to heal on the sabbath day? They held their peace. Which of you who had an ass, or an ox fallen into a pit would not straightaway pull him out on the sabbath day? And they could not answer him again.... (Lk. 14:1-6) And Jesus put forward a parable to those who were invited when he noticed how they chose their places of honor, saying to them, when you are invited to a wedding sit down not in the highest place lest a more honorable man than you was also invited; and he who invited you and him come and say to you give this man your place; and you, embarrassed, take the lowest place. But when you are invited go and sit down in the lowest place; so, when your host comes, he may say to you, friend go up higher: then you shall have status in the presence of the other guest. For whoever exalts himself shall be abased and he that humbles himself shall be exalted." (Lk. 14:7-11) If you host a dinner or supper, invite not just your friends or brother or kinsman or your rich neighbors so they invite you back; rather when you have a feast, invite the poor, the maimed, the blind; and you will be blessed; for they cannot repay you: for you will be rewarded at the resurrection of the just. (Lk. 14:12-14 only, except promotion/demotion: Mt. and Q.)

Luke here and elsewhere shows Jesus's disdain for the legalist ritual common among the Pharisees. He advocated for practical, compassionate action. Referring to proud, honor-seeking Jewish religious leaders, he advises individuals to be humble or to be embarrassed.

Jefferson believed that Jesus lived the example of generosity without expectation of reciprocity—that he embraced neighbors, countrymen, and all mankind with charity and philanthropy.

I'm certain that Jefferson, as governor, ambassador, vice president, and president, consistently received a place of honor and never sat humbly at the back of any room. Is that good, practical social advice for others not in his position?

It would be hard to believe that Jefferson followed such advice about inviting the poor to dinner, or traded votes or offered favors without expecting legislative repayment.

Jesus said to his disciples: A certain man made a great supper and invited many: and he sent his servant at supper time to tell them that they were invited. Come, for all things are now ready. And they all began to make excuses; the first said to him, I have bought a piece of ground and I must go and see it; I pray you, have me excused. And another said I have bought five yoke of oxen and I must go to test them; I pray you excuse me. And another said, I have married a wife and therefore I cannot come. So, the man's servant came and told his lord these things. Then, the master of the house being angry, said to his servant, go out quickly into the streets and lanes of the city, and bring me the poor, the maimed, the lame, and the blind. And the servant said, lord it is done as you have commanded, and yet there is still room. And the lord said to the servant go into the highway and byways and compel them to come in, that my house may be filled. For I say that none of those men who were invited and declined, shall taste my supper. (Lk. 14:16-24) For which of you intending to build a tower doesn't first sit down and consider the cost, whether he has sufficient funds to finish it? Lest after he had laid the foundation and is not able to finish it, all that observe it begin to mock him saying, this man began to build and was not able to finish. Or what king going to make war against another king doesn't sit down first and consider whether he would be able with ten thousand men, to meet the king that comes against him with twenty thousand? Or else while the other is yet a great distance away, he sends an ambassador to negotiate conditions of peace. (Lk. 14:28-32; also Mt., Th., and Q.)

Luke's is the most original of these similar parables. He reiterates Jesus's lesson that many are called but few (rich) are chosen.

Although Jefferson wasn't out of debt throughout his adult life, he was considered rich in his day. It's not clear what Jefferson's afterlife expectations were. He seemed to believe in a final judgement and assumed he had properly accepted and attended the "great supper," and had accepted the call to the Kingdom of Man.

The building of Monticello suggests that Jefferson understood the second parable message to finish what you start, but he seemed to also miss its lesson about properly planning and assuring sufficient funds to complete a project.

Then all the publicans and sinners drew near to hear Jesus. And the Pharisees and scribes murmured saying, this man receives sinners and eats with them. Jesus spoke this parable to them, what man having a hundred sheep if he loses one of them does not leave the ninety-nine in the wilderness and go after the one that is lost until he finds it? And when he finds it, he lays it on his shoulders rejoicing. And when he comes home, he calls together his friends and neighbors saying to them, rejoice with me for I have found my sheep which was lost. I say that likewise joy will be in heaven over one sinner that repents, more than over ninety-nine just persons who need no repentance. Either, that woman having ten pieces of silver, if she loses one piece does not light a candle and sweep the house and seek diligently until, she finds it? And when she's found it, she calls her friends and her neighbors together saying rejoice with me, for I have found a piece which I had lost. I say to you there is joy in the presence of angels of God over one sinner that repents. (Lk. 15:4-10; also Mt., Th., and Q.)

Luke described Jesus's attention to our individual importance and especially to the value of redeeming a single sinner.

Jefferson would recognize the message that Jesus cared about each and all of us imperfect mortals, yet the logical side of him would likely attend to the 99 "just persons" and delegate someone else to go find the missing one.

And Jesus said, a certain man had two sons; and the younger of them said to his father, father, give me my share of my inheritance. And the father did. After not many days the younger son gathered all his belongings and journeyed to a far country, and there he wasted his inheritance with riotous living. And when he had spent everything there arose mighty famine in that land; and he began to be in want. And he went to work for a citizen of that country who sent him into his fields to feed swine. And he would've been willing to fill his belly with the husks that the swine ate; and nobody helped him. And he realized that many of his father's hired servants had bread enough to spare and yet he would perish with hunger! He decided to go home to his father and will tell him, I have sinned against heaven and before him, and that I am no longer worthy to be called your son: hire me as one of your servants. And so, he returned home to his father. But when he was yet a great way off his father saw him and had compassion and ran and fell on his neck and kissed him. And the son said to him, father I have sinned against heaven and in your sight and I am no longer worthy to be called your son. But the father said to his servants, bring forth the best robe and put it on him; and put a ring on his hand and shoes on his feet and bring to me the fatted calf and kill it; and let's eat and be merry: for this is my son who was dead, and he's alive again; he was lost and is found. And they began to be merry. Now his elder son was in the field: and as he came close to the house, he heard music and dancing. And he called one of the servants and asked what these things meant. And the servant said to him, your brother has come home, and your father has killed the fatted calf, because he received him safe and sound. And he was angry and would not go in: then his father came out and entreated him. And he answered to his father, these many years I have served you and have not transgressed at any time your commandment: and yet you never gave me a feast that I might make merry with my friends: but as soon as your other son has come who has devoured his inheritance with harlots, you have killed the fatted calf for him. And he said to him, son, you have always been with me and all that I have is yours. Because he returned, we should make merry and be glad; for your brother was dead and he's alive again; and was lost and is found. (Lk. 15:11-32 only)

Luke's well-known Parable of the Prodigal Son has Jesus show that repentance and forgiveness are essential and always possible. He preaches that we shouldn't be jealous of another's good fortune.

These lessons would be familiar to Jefferson's early biblical upbringing in the Church of England, although he personally didn't experience a riotous early life.

And Jesus said also to his disciples, there was a certain rich man who had a steward who he accused of wasting his goods. He called him in to give an accounting saying he could no longer be his steward. The steward said to himself, what shall I do... I cannot dig, I'm too ashamed to beg. I'm resolved what to do, when I'm put out of my stewardship, that they may receive me into their houses. So, he called all his lord's debtors... (and offered each a discounted settlement offer for immediate payment). And the lord commended the unjust steward because he had done wisely: for the children of this world are in their generation wiser than the children of light. ...Make to yourselves friends of the mammon of unrighteousness; that when you fail, they may receive you into everlasting habitations. He who is faithful in that which is least is faithful also in much: and he who is unjust in the least is unjust also in much. If you have not been faithful in the unrighteous mammon, who will commit to your trust the true riches? And if you have not been faithful in that which is another man's, who shall give you that which is your own? No servant can serve two masters: for either he will hate the one, ad love the other; or else he will hold to one and despise the other. You cannot serve God and Mammon. (Lk. 16:1-13) And the Pharisees who were covetous, heard all these things: and they derided him. Jesus said to them, you justify yourselves before men; but God knows your hearts: for that which is highly esteemed among men is abomination in the sight of God. (Lk. 16:14-15) Whoever puts away his wife and marries another, commits adultery: and whoever marries her who has been put away commits adultery. (Lk. 16:18; also Mt., Th., for two masters plus Mk. on divorce)

Here, Luke has Jesus tell of an incompetent, dishonest, self-serving property manager offering a discount to collect this rich man's

outstanding debts—all to curry favor with the rich man's debtors and ensure the manager's next job move. None of this sounds like Jesus.

Jefferson would not have approved of the same acts from his own slave or employee, so it's a mystery why he favorably included this parable. Jefferson kinda-sorta attempted to serve God, and he certainly sought material wealth, so perhaps he was reminding himself of the *ideal* of serving the poor and not serving the goals of wealth and privilege.

Jesus told of a certain rich man who dressed in purple and fine linen and ate sumptuously every day: and there was a beggar named Lazarus who laid at this man's gate full of sores and hoped to be fed with the crumbs that fell from the rich man's table. Moreover, the dogs came and licked his sores. And so it happened that the beggar died and was carried by the angels into Abraham's bosom. The rich man also died and was buried; and in hell's torment, he lifted his eyes and saw Abraham far off with Lazarus in his bosom. And he cried and said, Father Abraham have mercy on me, and send Lazarus so he may dip the tip of his finger in water and cool my tongue; for I am tormented in this flame. But Abraham said, son remember that you in your lifetime received your good things and likewise Lazarus evil things: but now he is comforted, and you are tormented. And between us and you there is a great fixed gulf, so Lazarus cannot pass to you or you to us. Then the rich man said, I pray therefor Father that you would send Lazarus to my father's house: for I have five brethren; so that Lazarus may warn them lest they also come to this place of torment. Abraham said to him, they have Moses and the prophets; let them hear them. And the rich man said they haven't listened Father Abraham, but if they heard from one who had died, they would repent. Abraham said back to him, if they don't hear Moses and the prophets, neither will they be persuaded even though they hear from one who rose from the dead. (Lk. 16:19-31 only)

Luke cautions to listen and accept Jesus's word about kindness and generosity to receive your heavenly reward or fail to listen and act accordingly and you will be punished forever in the fires of hell. Luke here has Jesus preach of a *spiritual* heaven or hell afterlife when Jesus more likely taught love and compassion so as to be judged worthy of the coming of God's kingdom on *earth*. Jesus certainly advocated for the poor and dispossessed, but the lesson plays into the pattern of the church placating the poor throughout history, promising justice and a better spiritual existence only after you die.

Jefferson considered himself a materialist as opposed to a spiritualist and made scant reference to Moses and the Jewish scriptures. This passage seems another exception to Jefferson's general exclusion of angels and

miracles, but he did support equality and the right to human dignity (eventually) for all.

Then Jesus said to his disciples. It is impossible but that offenses (sins) will come, but woe to him through whom they come! It would be better for him that a millstone was hanged about his neck, and he cast into the sea, than he should offend one of these little ones. Take heed to yourselves: if your brother trespasses against you, rebuke him: and if he repents, forgive him. And if he trespasses against you seven times in a day, and seven times in a day turns again to you saying, I repent; you should forgive him. (Lk. 17:1-4; also Mt., Mk., and Q.) But which of you, having a servant plowing or feeding the cattle, will say to him when he comes from the field, go and sit down to eat? And will you not rather say to him, make ready my supper and serve me until I have eaten and drunk; and afterward you shall eat and drink? Does he thank that servant because he did the things that he was ordered to do? I believe not. So, you likewise, say, when you have done all those things for which you are commanded, say we have done that which is our duty to do. (Lk. 17:7-10 only)

Luke reports Jesus's lesson in duty, and especially forgiveness. Here, Jesus preaches gratitude and appreciation for the common working man.

It's unlikely that Jefferson showed appreciation or gratitude for the work of his slaves, though he reportedly treated some of his indentured household help well. Did he "thank that servant because he did the things that he was ordered to do? I believe not." Given the social order of the day, it's unlikely that even his favored slaves were ever invited to dinner.

And when the Pharisees demanded when the kingdom of God should come Jesus answered the kingdom of God comes not with our knowing. And as it was in the days of Noah, so shall it also be in the days of the Son of Man. They ate, drank, and married until the day came that Noah entered the ark, and the flood came and destroyed them all. Likewise, it was in the days of Lot; they ate, drank bought, sold, planted, and built. but that same day Lot left Sodom It rained fire and brimstone from heaven and destroyed them all. Even thus shall it be when the Son of Man is revealed. On that day, he who shall be on the housetop, and his stuff in the house, let him not come down to take it away: and he who is in the field, let him likewise not return back. Remember Lot's wife. Whoever shall seek to save his life shall lose it: and whoever shall lose his life shall preserve it. In that night there shall be two men in one bed; the one shall be taken, and the other shall be left. Two women shall be grinding together, the one shall be taken, and other left. Two men shall be in the field; the one shall be taken, and the other left. (Lk. 17:20, 26-37; also Mt. and Q.)

Luke has Jesus say that God's imperial rule is in your presence—right here, not some far away spiritual realm. This corresponds to Thomas 3:3: "The imperial rule is within you and is outside of you." Luke recounts Jesus's lesson about always being prepared. Oddly, Jefferson left out Lk. 17:21: "Neither shall they say, Lo here! or, lo there! for, behold, the kingdom of God is within you." This passage is key to Jesus's earthly, temporal view and validates his belief in a material versus a spiritual, soul-oriented Jesus.

Jefferson may have supported repentance but surely discounted the miracle of Noah's ark and flood rescue of the world's flora and fauna, and it's unlikely that he bought Lot's wife salt transformation or the Sodom reign of fire. He, of course, acknowledged the warning of untimely death since he experienced the unpredictability of death of his wife and four of their six children.

And he spoke a parable to them that men ought always to pray and not to faint; Saying, there was in a city a judge, which feared not God, nor regarded man: And there was a widow in that city, and she came to him saying, avenge me of my adversary. And he would not for a while: but afterward he said to himself, although I do not fear God or man: but because this widow troubles me, I will avenge her lest she continues to come and weary me. And the Lord said, hear what the unjust judge said. And shall not God avenge his own elect, who cry day and night to him, though he long bears with them? I tell you that he will avenge them speedily. Nevertheless, when the Son of Man comes, shall he find faith on earth? He spoke this parable to those certain in themselves, that they were righteous and despised others: (Lk. 18:1-8) Two men went to the temple to pray: the one a Pharisee, and the other publican. The Pharisee stood and prayed to himself, God, I thank you, that I am not like other men: extortioners, unjust, adulterers, or even like this publican. I fast twice a week I give tithes of all that I possess. And the publican, standing far off, would not so much as lift his eyes up to heaven but smote his breast, saying, God be merciful to me a sinner. The publican went to his house justified rather than the Pharisee; For everyone who exalts himself shall be abased; and he who humbles himself shall be exalted. (Lk. 18:10-14)

Luke likely copied these three passages from the hypothetical Q source and then added his own editorial musings. Don't faint, don't trust unjust judges or arrogant, ostentatious Pharisees, and be humble because we are all sinners. This is Luke's rendering of another of Jesus's jabs at the hypocritical, self-righteous, showboating religious leaders of the time who will get no

mercy, and his praise for the humble prayers of the repentant publican common man.

Jefferson experienced religious, hypocritical, only-for-show politicians, but he carefully maintained that his religion was between him and his God. Given his already exalted status, it's unlikely that he ever "humbled himself."

Now it came to pass that Jesus entered a certain village: and a certain woman named Martha received him into her house. And she had a sister called Mary who also sat at Jesus' feet and heard his word. But Martha was much encumbered about serving, and came to him, and said, Lord, do you not care that my sister has left me to serve alone? Bid her therefore that she helps me. Jesus answered, Martha, you are careful and troubled about many things. But one thing is most needed: and Mary has chosen that good part, which shall not be taken away from her. (Lk. 10:38-42)

This Luke-only passage is intended as an admonition to focus on the importance and value of listening to spiritual advice.

Jesus departed from Galilee and came to the coasts of Judea beyond Jordan. And great multitudes followed him. The Pharisees also came, tempting him asking, is it lawful for a man to put away his wife for every cause? Jesus answered, Have you not read that in the beginning he made them male and female, and for this cause shall a man leave father and mother and cleave to his wife: and the two shall be one flesh? .... What therefore God has joined together, let not man put asunder. The Pharisees said, why did Moses then command to give a writing of divorce, and to put her away? Jesus said, Moses, because of the hardness of your hearts, suffered you to put away your wives: but from the beginning it was not so. I say to you, whosoever shall put away his wife, except for fornication, and shall marry another, commits adultery: and whosoever marries her who is put away also commits adultery. His disciples said to Jesus, if the case of the man be so with his wife, it is not good to marry. He responded, all men cannot receive this saying, save those to whom it is given. For there are some eunuchs, which were so born of heaven's sake. He who is able to receive it, let him receive it. (Mt. 19:1-12) Then little children were brought to Jesus so that he would touch and bless them but those who brought them were rebuked by the disciples. But Jesus said, don't discourage or inhibit little children from coming to me, for they are the kingdom of heaven. He did lay his hands on them and departed. (Mt. 19:13-15; also Mk. and Lk.)

Matthew's version follows Judean law for his Jewish audience and doesn't jibe with an earlier Mark version, which has Jesus recite Roman

law. Two hundred years after Jefferson, divorce (and adultery) is largely settled by civil law, not Christian religious laws.

Jesus may have meant his words to children also to include the poor and dispossessed. To Jefferson, this likely meant that the humility and innocence of little children is the ideal spiritual attitude.

And Jesus had a man come up and ask, Master what good thing shall I do that I may have eternal life? and Jesus said to him, why do you call me good? There is none good but one that is God. But to enter into life, keep the commandments. The man said to him, which? Jesus said, you shall not commit murder, nor commit adultery, nor steal, nor bear false witness. Honor the father and your mother and love your neighbor as yourself. The young man replied, all these commandments I have kept from my youth. What do I still lack? Jesus said, if you will be perfect, go and sell all that you have and give it to the poor and you shall have treasure in heaven. And then come and follow me. But when the young man heard that he went away sorrowful for he had many possessions. And then Jesus said to his disciples that a rich man shall hardly enter the kingdom of heaven for it is easier for a camel to go through the eye of a needle than for a rich man to enter into the kingdom of God. When the disciples heard this, they were amazed saying who then could be saved. But Jesus said, with man alone this is impossible but with God all things are possible. (Mt. 19:16-26; also Mk. 10:17-22 and Lk. 18:18-23)

A common early Christian belief was that attachment to material things impeded the development of kindness and compassion. This common wisdom was often expressed in the writings of the evangelists. The Jesus Seminar thought it unlikely that this lesson was spoken by Jesus—that is, the promise of heavenly reward for making oneself poor. The passage likely appealed to the early Christian leaders as incentive to financially support the church.

Jefferson, a rich man, apparently assumed that he had kindness and compassion and could therefore pass through the "eye of a needle" to enter the kingdom of God.

The kingdom of heaven is like a householder who, early in the morning hired laborers to work in his vineyard for a penny a day. About three hours later he saw idle men in the marketplace and hired them for whatever salary is right. He did the same six and nine hours later asking why the men were idle and offered them whatever was right. At the end of the day, he instructed his steward to pay them, last to first. Those hired last were given a penny leading those hired first to expect more; but they likewise received a penny. They complained saying that the last hired only worked one hour but were paid equal to us. The householder answered one saying, he did them no wrong since the men had agreed to work the day for a penny. Take what we agreed and go your way. Is it not lawful for me to do what I wish with what is mine? Is your eye evil because I am good? So, the last shall be first, and the first last: for many are called but few are chosen. (Mt. 20:1-16 only; last shall be first: also Mk., Lk., Th., and Q.)

This parable, unique to Matthew and likely attributable to Jesus, aligns with Jesus's tendency to favor the poor (those last-in laborers). This theme of many being called but few chosen repeats throughout the gospels.

Jefferson seemed likely to apportion reward for work based on time and effort. He apparently believed in an ultimate judgment but not in the concept of a soul to judge.

And Jesus entered and passed through Jericho. There he met a rich man named Zacharias, who was the chief among the publicans (Roman public tax collectors) and who wanted to see this man Jesus. But because he was small and because of the press of the crowd he could not see him. So, he ran ahead and climbed a sycamore tree because he knew Jesus would pass that way.

When Jesus did pass, he looked up, saw him, and said to him, Zacchaeus, quickly come down because today I must visit your house. He hurried down and received Jesus joyfully. And when the crowd saw this, they all murmured that Jesus was going to be a guest of a man who is a sinner. Zacchaeus stood and said to the Lord, half of my possessions I give to the poor; and if I have taken anything by a false accusation from any man, I restore to him fourfold. Jesus told him, this day salvation has come to this house for this man is also a son of Abraham. For the son of man comes to seek and to save those who were lost. (Lk. 19:1-10 only)

Luke likely copied a common proverb and attributed it to Jesus to make the point that it's important in life to act kindly and generously, and that mere dogmatic belief or observing prescribed ritual doesn't lead to the kingdom of God.

Jefferson supported states' rights and opposed all but minimal federal taxation. He supported well-off individual farm and plantation owners, but also stood for underdog non-landowners' rights. Maybe Jefferson took solace in these words since Luke shows that Jesus, uncharacteristically, didn't discount this rich man and indicated that he, too, could be saved.

Jesus spoke a parable as he neared Jerusalem and because his disciples thought that the kingdom of God should immediately appear. He said, a Nobleman traveled a far country to receive a kingdom and return. Upon departing he gave his servants each ten pounds to invest while he was away. But his citizens hated him and sent a message after him saying, we will not have this man rule over us. And when the man received his kingdom and returned, he called his servants to account for the money he had given them. The first reported he had gained ten pounds and he said to him, well done good servant, because you have been faithful, you will have authority over ten cities. And the second came saying, lord, your pound has earned five pounds. Likewise, he said to him, you have authority over five cities. And another came and said, lord here is your pound which I have kept wrapped up in a napkin: for I feared you, being an austere man: you take up what you don't lay down and reap what you do not sow. The lord said to him, by your own words will I judge you, you wicked servant; you knew I required my own with usury. He said to those around, take his servant's pound and give it to he who has ten pounds. I say, to everyone who has, more shall be given; and from him who has little, even that will be taken away. But my enemies who will that I not reign over them, bring them here and slay them before me. After he spoke this parable, Jesus went to Jerusalem. (Lk. 19:11-28; also Mk. and Mt.)

The Jesus Seminar considers this Luke parable, originally intended to show Jesus's departure and return, to be "highly edited" by the early Christian community, then copied by Luke and Matthew. A man goes on a trip, entrusts his money to his three slaves, then returns to hold them to account. Two slaves who turned a profit are rewarded, the third who hid the money in a napkin was chastised, and his money given to the slave who made the greatest profit.

Jefferson included this parable in his Bible, but I wonder why, because "...to everyone who has, more will be given; and from those who don't have, even what they do have will be taken away" doesn't sound like Jesus. Jefferson may have appreciated the entrepreneurial lesson and the advice to use your God-given talents wisely or they'll be lost. It's doubtful that Luke, through Jesus, intended this passage as an argument for capitalism.

When Jesus and his disciples neared Mount Olives on the way to Jerusalem..., Jesus sent two disciples to find and bring back a donkey and a colt. If any object, tell them that the Lord needs them, and they will send them. They went and did as Jesus commanded and brought back the animals and set Jesus on the donkey. Many in the multitudes spread their cloaks and tree branches ahead of his procession. When Jesus arrived in

Jerusalem, the whole city was moved to ask Who is this man? (Mt. 21:1-10; Mk. 11:1-11; Lk. 19:29-40; OT Zech. 9:9; Ps. 118:26) The Pharisees said among themselves, we have not prevailed; the world has welcomed him. And there were certain Greeks among them that came to worship at the feast.... I say to you, except a kernel of wheat fall into the ground and die, it abides alone: but if it dies, it brings forth much fruit. (J. 12:19-24) Jesus then left and lodged overnight in nearby Bethany. (Mt. 21:17)

Matthew and Luke copy Mark's account conceived to make Jesus's entry into Jerusalem fit and fulfil the Hebrew scriptures' prophecies of Zechariah 9:9 and Psalm 118:26. They used this grand entrance as an opening narrative to set the stage for Jesus's final fate. John then adds the farming lore saying that only by sowing one apparently dead seed can new plant life grow and produce many more. He suggests that the death of Jesus is for the benefit of many in mankind.

Jefferson likely associated this passage with his experience that British and French monarchies had to die before the American Revolution could produce new fruits of freedom and reform.

The next day, returning from Bethany, Jesus went to the temple and expelled those who bought and sold there. He tipped over the moneychangers' tables and the chairs of those who sold doves and would not accept that men should carry containers through the temple. He taught, is it not written that all nations shall call my house be a house of prayer? But you have made it a den of thieves. The scribes and chief priests heard him and plotted to destroy him. They now feared him because of how the people had been astonished at his doctrine. Jesus left that evening but returned to the temple the next day... and again met with the chief priests, the scribes, and the elders. (Mk. 11:12, 15-19, 27; also Mt., Lk., and J.)

Mark shows Jesus committed to act to correct the abuses and materialism of Judaism while accepting great personal risk. Reform of the abuses of Judaism of his day is the essence of Jesus's intended short public mission. He took over and propagated the message of the more popular but imprisoned and then beheaded John the Baptist.

Jefferson risked actively opposing autocratic British rule then encouraged and advanced a new free republic. He (privately) criticized the distortions and failings that he saw in the Bible and Christianity then promoted a reason-based Christianity with his own Bible.

Having returned to the temple, Jesus asks, what do you think? A man had two sons and told the first, son, go to work today in my vineyard. The son said, I will not: but afterward repented and went. He told the second son the same who answered, I go, sir, but did not go. Jesus asked, which of the two did the will of the father? Those in the temple answered, the first. Jesus responded, ... The publicans and harlots (like the first son) go into the kingdom of God before you. (Mt. 21:28-31 only)

Through Matthew, Jesus again criticizes the priests, scribes, and elders as hypocrites for saying and promising charity and obedience to the commandments but living a privileged life. They say that they will abide by the Jewish law, yet they don't.

We can suppose that Jefferson would favor the positive action of the first son.

Jesus told another parable: A man planted a vineyard, planted a surrounding hedge, dug a place for a wine vat, built a tower, leased it all to operators and left to far away. At the end of the growing season, the man sent his servant to the operators to collect the fruit of the vineyard. The operators caught and beat the servant and sent him back empty handed. The man sent another servant who the operators shamefully stoned, wounded in the head, and sent him back. The man sent others, some they beat and others they killed. Finally, the man sent his beloved only son feeling sure they would respect him. But the operators said among themselves, this is the heir, let's kill him and the inheritance will be ours. They took and killed him and tossed his body out of the vineyard. What should the lord of the vineyard do? He should go and destroy the operators and give the vineyard to others. (Mk. 12:1-9) When the chief priests and Pharisees heard this parable, they knew that it was about them. But when they sought to arrest him, they feared the crowd of his supporters who saw Jesus as a prophet. (Mt. 21:45, 46; also Th. 65:1-7, Mt. 21:33-39, and Lk. 20:9-15)

Thomas's gospel may have first reported this common early Christian Jesus saying, which Thomas concluded with the killing of the owner's son. Later gospel writers thought the parable incomplete and, like here, added their own conclusions. At this late point in his public life, Jesus more openly and directly criticized the Pharisees, scribes, and the corrupt religious establishment.

To Jefferson and later scholars, this Mark passage likely signified the transfer of God's favor from Israel to nascent gentile Christianity.

Jesus said, the kingdom of God is like a certain king which made a marriage for his son and sent his servants to call guests to the wedding, and they would not come. Again, he sent forth other servants to tell the invited guest, I have prepared my dinner: my oxen and fatted calf are killed, and all things are ready: come to the marriage. But they made light of it, and went their ways, one to his farm, another to his merchandise: and others treated his servant spitefully and slew them. But when the king heard of this, he was angry: and he sent his armies, and destroyed those murderers and burned their city. Then he told his servants, the wedding is ready and those invited were not worthy. Go therefore to the highways and whoever you find, invite to the marriage. So, the servants went and gathered as many as they found, both good and bad: and the wedding was furnished with guests. And when the king came in to see the guests, he saw a man not dressed in a wedding garment and said to him, friend, how come you came here not having a wedding garment, and the man was speechless. Then the king told his servants to bind him hand and foot, take him away and cast him into outer darkness; there shall be weeping and gnashing of teeth. For many are called, but few are chosen. (Mt. 22:1-14; also, Lk. 14:16-24, Th. 42, and Q.?)

Thomas's original version ended with the host's subsequent invitation to anyone on the streets, whereas Luke had the host invite the poor, the blind, the crippled, and the lame, which seems more like something that the historical Jesus would do. Jefferson picked Matthew's gospel parable, the harshest of the two then-known versions, with Matthew's host being a king

(God) preparing a feast for his son (Jesus) and being rejected by the guests (Israel) who are destroyed like Jerusalem. Each gospel version includes the lesson that many are called but few are chosen; the privileged wealthy (Jewish religious leaders) are called, and common folks (Christians) are chosen.

Jefferson professed that all men are created equal, but social and economic life in his day only designated free white landowners as the earthly chosen.

Attempting to entangle Jesus, the Pharisees sent their disciples saying, master, we know you are true and teach the way of God, not caring for the teachings of men. So, tell us: Is it lawful or not to pay tribute to Caesar? But Jesus perceived their trap and asked, why do you tempt me you hypocrites? Show me the tribute money, and they brought him a coin. Whose image is on this coin? They answered, Caesar's. Jesus then told them, render to Caesar the things which are Caesar's; and to God, the things that are God's. They marveled at his answer and left. (Mt. 22:15-22) The same day Sadducees, which say there is no resurrection, said to Jesus, Master, Moses said, if a man dies having no children, his brother shall marry his wife and raise up seed to his brother. Now, there were seven brethren: and the first married a wife had no children and died and left his wife to his brother: likewise, the second also and the third, unto the seventh. Last the wife died. Therefore, in the resurrection, whose wife shall she be of the seven? for they all had her. Jesus answered, you err, not knowing the scriptures, nor the power of God. For in the resurrection, they neither marry, nor are given in marriage, but are as the angels of heaven. ... have you not read that which was spoken by God, who said, I am the God of Abraham, and the God of Isaac, and the God of Jacob? God is not the God of the dead, but of the living. When the multitude heard this, they were astonished at his doctrine. (Mt. 22:23-27, 29-33; also Mk., Lk., and Th.)

Matthew (and others) show how the Pharisees continually attempted to trap Jesus into a punishable heresy by having him contradict Jewish law teachings.

Jefferson probably appreciated how Jesus parried the political-like verbal attacks of the Pharisees with his rational response to their legalistic questions. Jefferson criticized this same nitpicking in subsequent Christian theology, dogma, and ritual that he saw going far astray of the simple teachings of Jesus.

One of the scribes came and seeing that Jesus had reasoned and answered well, asked him, which is the first commandment of them all? Jesus answered him, the first of all the commandments is, Hear O Israel: The Lord our God is one Lord: and you shall love the Lord your God with all your soul, and with all your mind, and with all your strength. The second commandment is: you shall love your neighbor as yourself. There is no other commandment greater than these. (Mk. 12:28-31) On these two commandments hang all the law and prophets. (Mt. 22:40) And the scribe said to him, well master you have said the truth: for there is one God; and there is none other than he: And to love him with all the heart and with the understanding, with all the soul, and with all the strength, and to love his neighbor as himself, is worth more than all the burnt offerings and sacrifices. (Mk. 12:32-33; also Mt. and Lk.)

Mark reported Jesus's baseline message: Love god, and especially, love your neighbor as yourself.

Jefferson would recognize this as classic spiritual advice in virtually all the world's great religions. Jefferson likely picked this passage believing that this is all that we need to know to live a successful spiritual life.

And to the crowd and his disciples he said: The scribes and Pharisees sit in Moses' seat: Observe their words but not their acts, for they say, and do not. They lay on men grievous and heavy burdens, but they won't lift a finger to carry these burdens. They act only to be observed by other men. They display their parchment holy verses and wear orthodox garments. They assume places of honor at feasts and take the chief seats at the synagogues. They seek greetings in the marketplace to be called: Rabbi, Rabbi. So, don't you seek to be called Rabbi for Christ is your master and all are your brethren. And on earth, call no man father for your Father is in heaven. And don't be called master, for Christ is your master. But he who is greatest among you shall be your servant, and whosoever shall exalt himself shall be abased; and he that shall humble himself shall be exalted. But woe unto you, scribes and pharisees hypocrites! For you shut up the kingdom of heaven against men: for you neither go in yourselves, neither suffer you them that are entering to go in. Woe to you scribes and Pharisees, Hypocrites! For you devour widows' houses, and for a pretense make a long prayer: therefore, you shall be dammed. Woe unto you, scribes and Pharisees, hypocrites! For you travel sea and land to make one proselyte, and when he is made, you make him twofold more the child of hell than yourselves. Woe unto you, you blind guides who say, whosoever shall swear by the temple it is nothing; but whosoever shall swear by the gold of the temple, he is a debtor. You are fools and blind! For which is greater, the gold or the temple that sanctifies the gold? And whosoever shall swear by the alter, it is nothing;

but whosoever swears by the gift upon it is guilty. You are fools and blind! For which is greater, the gift or the alter that sanctifies the gift? ...so, swear by the altar and the temple... and he who swears by heaven swears by the throne of God and by He who sits upon it. Woe unto you, scribes and Pharisees, hypocrites! For you tithe mint, and anise, and cumin, and have omitted the weightier matters of the law, judgement, mercy, and faith: these you ought to have done and not leave the other undone. You blind guides! Who strain at a gnat and swallow a camel. And woe to you scribes and Pharisees, hypocrites, for you clean the outside of the cup and platter, but within are extortion and excess; cleanse first what is inside the cup and platter that the outside of them may be clean also. Woe unto you, scribes and Pharisees, hypocrites! for you are like white sepulchers, which appear beautiful outside, but within are full of dead men's bones, and of uncleanness. Outwardly you appear righteous to men but inside you are full of hypocrisy and iniquity. Woe unto you, scribes and Pharisees, hypocrites! Because you build the tombs of the prophets and garnish the sepulchers of the righteous. And say, if we had been in the days of our fathers, we would not have been partaken with them in the blood of the prophets. Wherefore, you be witness to yourself, that you are the children of those who killed the prophets. Accept the judgement of your fathers. You serpents, you generation of vipers! How can you escape the damnation of hell? (Mt. 23:1-33; also Mk. and Lk.)

Matthew tells us what he really thought, as he had Jesus in uncharacteristically harsh language, rail against the abuses of some of the Jewish religious leaders of his day—namely, how we should judge them by their actions, not by their holy words. In all the gospels, Jesus is shown as a classic reformer activist.

It's safe to say that Jefferson encountered his share of political hypocrites whose actions belied their words.

And Jesus noticed how people contributed alms for the poor and that the rich contributed a great amount. Along came a poor widow and she threw in just two coins. Jesus remarked to his disciples that this poor woman contributed more than the rich because they gave from their abundance, but she gave from poverty, all that she had for her to live on. (Mk. 12:41-44; also Lk.)

Mark has Jesus tell us that it's not the amount but your attitude and sacrifice in giving that's important.

Jefferson would have likely fit the stereotype of the rich person who gives from abundance, though he probably also admired the principle of sacrifice. He's commonly quoted as saying: "May I never get too busy in my own affairs that

I fail to respond to the needs of others with kindness and compassion." Of course, his charitable giving may have sometimes been with borrowed funds.

Jesus departed from the temple and Jesus said to his disciples of the temple building: There shall not be left here one stone upon another, that shall not be thrown down. (Mt. 24:1-2) Let those who are in Judea flee to the mountains: let he who is on the house top not come down to take things out of his house: Neither let he who is in the field return back to take his clothes. And woe to those who are with child and to those who are nursing in those days. But pray you that your flight be not in the winter, neither on the sabbath day: for then shall be great tribulations such as was not since the beginning of the world to this time, no, nor ever shall be. (Mt. 24:16-21) Immediately after the tribulation of those days shall the sun be darkened, and the moon shall not give her light, and the stars shall fall from heaven, and the powers of heaven shall be shaken. (Mt. 24:29; also Mk. and Lk.) Now learn a parable of the fig tree; when its branch is yet tender and puts forth leaves you know that summer is near: likewise, when you shall see all these things, know that it is near even at the door. (Mt. 24:32-33) But when that day comes no man knows, no not the angels of heaven, but my Father only. But, as in the days of Noah, so shall it also be at the coming of the Son of Man. For in the days before the flood, they were eating, drinking, marrying, and giving in marriage, until the day that Noah entered the ark, and they didn't know until the flood came and took them all away; then shall two be in the field; and one shall be taken and the other left. Two women shall be grinding at the mill; the one shall be taken and the other left. Watch therefore: for you know not what hour your Lord will come. But know this, that if the good man of the house had known in what hour the thief would come, he would have watched and would not have suffered his house to be broken up. Therefore, be you also ready: who then is a faithful and wise servant, whom his Lord had made ruler over his household to give them meat in due season? Blessed is that servant whom his Lord when he comes shall find so doing. I say to you, that he should make him ruler over all of his goods. But if that evil servant shall say in his heart, my lord delays his coming; and shall begin to smite his fellow servants, and to eat and drink with the drunken; the Lord of that servant shall come in a day and in an hour when the servant doesn't expect him, and shall cut him asunder, and appoint him his portion with the hypocrites: there shall be weeping and gnashing of teeth. (Mt. 24:36-51; also Mk. and Lk.) Then shall the kingdom of heaven be like ten virgins, who took their lamps and went to meet the bridegroom. Five of them were wise, and five were foolish. Those who were foolish took their lamps and took no oil with them: but the wise took oil in containers along with their lamps. While the bridegroom tarried, they all slumbered and slept, and at midnight there was a cry, behold, the bride groom comes; go out to meet him. All the virgins arose and trimmed their lamps. And the foolish said to the wise, give us your oil, for our lamps have gone out. But the wise answered saying, not so; lest there not be enough for us and you: but go rather to those who sell and buy oil for yourselves. And while they went to buy, the bride groom came; and those who were ready went in with him to the marriage: and the door was shut. Afterwards, the other virgins came, saying Lord, Lord, open to us. But he answered and said, I don't know you. (Mt. 25:1-12) Watch, therefore. For the kingdom of heaven is as a man traveling to a far country, who called his own servants and delivered to them his goods. To one he gave five talents, two another two, and to another one; to every man according to his ability; and left on his journey. Then he who had received five talents went and treated with the same and earned another five talents. And he who had received two, also gained another two. But he who had received one, dug in the Earth and hid his lord's money. After a long time, the Lord of those servants came back and reckoned with them. And so, he who had received five talents came and brought him another five talents saying, lord you gave me five talents: behold I have gained another five talents. His lord said, well done, you good and faithful servant: you have been faithful over a few things, I will make you ruler over many things: enter you into the joy of your Lord. He also who received two talents came and said lord, you gave me two talents: I have gained two other talents beside them. His Lord said to him, well done good and faithful servant; you have been faithful over a few things, I will make you ruler over many things: enter you into the joy of your Lord. Then he who had received the one talent came and said, lord, I know that you are a hard man, reaping where you have not sown and gathering where you have not harvested, and I was afraid and went and hid your talent in the earth: here then is what you gave me. His lord answered and said to him, you wicked and slothful serving, you know that I reap where I sowed not and gathered where I have not harvested; you should therefore have put my money to the exchangers, and then at my coming I should have received my own with usury. Therefore, take the talent from him and give it to he who has 10 talents. For to everyone who has, shall be given, and he shall have abundance: but from he who has not shall be taken away even that which he has. And cast the unprofitable servant into outer darkness: there shall be weeping and gnashing of teeth. (Mt. 25:13-30; same lesson as Lk. 19:12-27 and Q.?) And take heed to yourselves, lest at any time your hearts be overcharged with overeating, drunkenness, and cares of this life and so that day come upon you unaware. For as a snare shall it come on all of them that dwell on this earth. Watch therefore and pray always that you may be accounted worthy to escape all these things that shall come to pass, and to stand before the Son of Man. (Lk. 21:34-36)

These parables speak to the end of times—judgement day which will come as a surprise. Again, these are lessons about using your talents, reaping what you sow, and the dangers of a wasteful and unproductive life.

Miraculous apocalypse, maybe not, but Jefferson apparently believed in a final judgement and perhaps an afterlife. He knew from life experience that death often came unannounced—so be prepared. He could certainly identify with being judged in public, often harshly and unexpectedly.

When the Son of Man shall come in his glory, and all the holy angels with him, then shall he sit upon the throne of his glory: and before him shall be gathered all nations: and he shall separate them one from another, as a shepherd divides his sheep from the goats: and he shall set the sheep on his right hand, but the goats on the left. Then shall the King say to them on his right hand, come you blessed of my Father, inherit the kingdom prepared for you from the foundation of the world: For I was hungry, and you gave me food: I was thirsty, and you gave me drink: I was a stranger, and you took me in: naked, and you clothed me: I was sick, and you visited me: I was in prison, and you came to me. Then will the righteous answer him, saying Lord, when did we see you hungry or thirsty or sick or homeless or imprisoned or without clothes? Or when did we see you sick or in prison and came to you? And the King shall he answer them and say, as you have done these things to the poor and suffering of your brethren, you have done it for me. Then he will say to those on his left hand, depart from me, you cursed into everlasting fire, prepared for the devil and his angels: for I hungered, and you gave me no food: I was thirsty, and you gave me no drink: I was a stranger, and you did not take me in: naked, and you clothed me not: sick, and in prison, and you visited me not. Then they shall also answer him saying, Lord, when did we see you as hungry, or thirsty, or a stranger, or naked, or sick, or in prison, and did not minister to you? He answered, inasmuch as you did it not to one of the least, you did it not to me. And these shall go into everlasting punishment: but the righteous into life eternal. (Mt. 25:31-46 only)

Matthew wrote of Jesus's teaching us to show compassion to all our fellow earth travelers, especially those in need, as if we were showing compassion to Jesus.

Jefferson reportedly treated his slaves well, but surely, only freeing them would have qualified as righteous behavior under this parable. It seems that Jefferson believed in his heart that all men are created equal and even tried in his youth to introduce at least eventual

emancipation. But having been rebuffed, and due to social and political pressures and the need for compromise to establish and maintain the new republic, he eventually accepted the status quo and hoped for eventual abolishment of slavery.

Two days before the feast of Passover, the chief priests and the scribes plotted how they might capture and kill Jesus. But they said not on the feast day, lest there be an uproar of the people. And being in Bethany, in the house of Simon the leper, as Jesus ate a meal, a woman came with an alabaster box of precious ointment, she broke open the box and poured it on his head. Some indignant bystanders said among themselves, why was this ointment wasted? For it might have been sold for more than three hundred pence and have been given to the poor. And they murmured against her. Jesus said, let her alone, why do you trouble her? She wrought a good work on me. For you have the poor with you always, and whensoever you will, you may do them good: but me you have not always. She did what she could: she came beforehand to anoint my body before burying. (Mk. 14:1-8) Then, one of the twelve, Judas Iscariot, went to the chief priests and asked, what will you give me to deliver Jesus to you? And they agreed to give him thirty pieces of silver. From that time forward, Judas sought a time and place to betray Jesus. (Mt. 26:14-16; also Lk.)

Mark and all the gospel writers depict Jesus as a reformer who was apparently successful enough that the Pharisees thought him a threat to their privileged positions and livelihood. A plot to eliminate him and do it at a less public time are both believable. Judas's betrayal seems a metaphor, since we have no evidence that, if this Judas existed, that he could or would have turned on Jesus. Certainly, a Zealot, Judas-type betrayer could have been encouraged, and even paid, by the Pharisees or scribes to help them eliminate a heretic to the established Jewish religious order. Historically, the Romans, not the Jews, convicted and executed Jesus for treason.

Politically, Jefferson doubtlessly experienced intrigue and potential betrayal during his time in politics and could relate to the Judas syndrome.

Now on the first day of the feast of unleavened bread, the disciples came to Jesus asking him, where would you like us to prepare for you to eat Passover. And he said, go to the city to such a man and say to him, the Master said, my time is at hand; I will keep the Passover at your house with my disciples. And the disciples did as Jesus had appointed them; and they made ready the Passover. Now when the evening had come, he sat down with the twelve. (Mt. 26:17-20) And there was strife among them, which of them should be accounted the greatest, and he said to them, the kings of the Gentiles exercise lordship over them; and they who exercise authority over them are called benefactors. But you shall not be so: but he who is the greatest among you, let him be as the younger: and he that is chief, as he who serves. For which is greater, he who sits to eat, or he who serves? Is it not he that sits to eat? But I am among you as he who serves. (L. 22:24-27) And supper having ended, Jesus rose from the meal and laid aside his garments and took a towel and girded himself. After that he poured water into a basin and began to wash the disciple's feet and to wipe them with the towel. Then he came to Simon Peter: and Peter said to him, Lord do you wash my feet? Jesus answered and said to him, what I do now, you don't know now; but you shall know hereafter. Peter said to him, you shall never wash my feet. Jesus answered him, if I wash you not, you have no part with me. Simon Peter said to him, Lord not my feet only, but also my hands and my head. Jesus said to him, he who is washed need not save to wash his feet but he's clean everywhere, and you are clean, but not all. For he knew who would betray him; therefore, he said, you are not all clean. So, after he had washed their feet and taken his garments and sat down again, he said to them, do you know what I have done to you? You call me master and Lord: and you say well, for so I am. If I then, your Lord and Master, have washed your feet, you also ought to wash one another's feet. For I have given you an example, that you should do as I have done to you. I say to you, the servant is not greater than his Lord: neither he that is sent, greater than he who sent him. If you know these things, happy are you if you do them. (J. 13:2, 4-17) Jesus was troubled and said one of you twelve will betray me. The disciples then looked at one another wondering of whom he spoke. Now leaning on Jesus' bosom was one of his disciples, whom Jesus loved. Simon Peter beckoned to him that he should ask of whom Jesus spoke. He asked, Lord who is it? Jesus answered it is he to whom I shall give the sop when I have dipped it. He dipped his bread and gave it to Judas Iscariot, the son of Simon. (J. 13:21-26) When Judas departed, Jesus gave those remaining a new commandment: Love one another as I have loved you; by this love, all men will know you as my disciples. (J. 13:31, 34, 35; like last supper: Mk. 14:22-25, Mt. 26:29, and Lk. 22:15-20)

John uses "Lord and Master" Jesus's final meeting and washing of his disciples' feet as a dramatic example of Jesus's humility, service, and sacrifice. It's John's alternative to the institution of the Eucharist at Jesus's last supper as related by writers Mark, Matthew, and Luke. This event isn't known historically, though a meal gathering of disciples or loved ones during Passover would be a likely event. The idea of bread and wine representing Jesus's body and blood is fundamental to Christian worship to this day.

Jefferson didn't believe in the miracle of transubstantiation—that is, the communion host and wine being consecrated into Jesus's actual body and blood.

Jesus then said to them, all of you shall be offended (accused/assailed) because of me this night: Peter answered, though all men shall be offended because of you, I will never be offended. (Mt. 26:31, 33) I am ready to go with you into prison and to death. And Jesus said, Peter, the cock shall not crow this day before you will thrice deny that you know me. (Lk. 22:33, 34) Peter said to him, though I should die with you, yet I will not deny you. Likewise, also said all the disciples. Jesus then went with them to a place called Gethsemane and told the disciples, sit here while I go and pray yonder. He took with him Peter and the two sons of Zebedee and began to be sorrowful and very heavy. He then said, my soul is exceedingly sorrowful, even unto death: stay here and watch with me. Jesus went a little further, fell on his face and prayed, saying, O my Father, if it is possible, let his cup pass from me: nevertheless, not as I will, but as you will. He came back to the disciples, found them asleep and said to Peter, what! could you not watch with me for one hour? Watch and pray, that you enter not into temptation: the spirt indeed is willing, but the flesh is weak. He went away a second time, and prayed, saying, O my Father, if this cup may not pass away from me unless I drink it, your will be done. And he came back and found them asleep again: for their eyes were heavy. And he left them and went away again and prayed a third time saying the same words. Then he came back to his disciples and said to them, sleep on now and take your rest. (Mt. 26:35-45; also Mk. and J.)

This passage suggests that even the most dedicated and ostensibly loyal supporter is weak when asked to do a difficult task—that we all are human and prone to failure.

Jefferson surely knew in spirit to abide by the good book and was known to be loyal and true while married. Yet, like all of us, his flesh was weak, especially as to a good friend's wife and to his relations with slave Sally Hemings, his departed wife's half-sister.

Jesus went with his disciples over the brook Cedron and entered a garden. And Judas, who was to betray him, also knew the place: for Jesus often went there with his disciples. Judas, having joined with a band of men and officers from the chief priests and Pharisees, came there with lanterns, torches, and weapons. (J. 18:1-3) Judas gave this group a sign saying, whomever I kiss, that will be Jesus, hold him fast. And Judas came to Jesus and said, hail Master, and kissed him. And Jesus said, friend, why have you come? (Mt. 26:48-50) Jesus, knowing all things, went forward and asked, whom do you seek? They answered, Jesus of Nazareth, and Jesus said I am he. When he said this, Judas and the group went backward and fell to the ground. Then Jesus asked again, whom do you seek? They answered, Jesus of Nazareth. Jesus answered, I have told you, I am he, therefore let these others go their way. (J. 18:4-8) Then they came and laid hands on Jesus and took him. One of Jesus' disciples drew his sword and struck a servant of the high priest severing his ear. Jesus said to his disciple, put your sword in its place: for all who take up the sword shall perish with the sword. Then Jesus said to the multitudes, are you come out as against a thief with swords and staves to take me? I sat daily with you teaching in the temple, and you laid no hold on me. Then all his disciples forsook him and fled. (Mt. 26:50-52, 55-56) And a certain young man followed him, having a linen cloth about his naked body: and the young men grabbed him. He left behind the linen cloth and fled from them naked. (Mk. 14:51-52) And they that laid hold on Jesus led him away to Caiaphas the high priest, where the scribes and elders were assembled. (Mt. 26:57) And Simon Peter followed Jesus, as did another disciple, who was known to the high priest, and he went in with Jesus to the palace of the high priest. But Peter stayed at the door until the other disciple came and brought Peter in. Peter stood with the servants and officers in the cold. They had made a fire, and all warmed themselves. Then the woman who kept the door asked Peter, are you not one of this man's disciples? Peter said, I am not. Simon Peter stood and warmed himself and another asked, Are you not one of his disciples? He denied it and said I am not. One of the servants, kin to the man whose ear was cut off, said, did I not see you in the garden with him? Peter then denied again: and immediately the cock crowed. (J. 18:15-16, 18-17, 25-27) Peter remembered the words of Jesus who had said to him, before the cock crows, you will deny me three times, and he went out and wept bitterly. (Mt. 26:75; also Mk. and Lk.)

It seems likely that Jesus had been arrested, as reported in all the gospels, and he may have said, "All who take up the sword shall perish with the sword," yet no one knows the historic details of his arrest. More likely, these passages are lessons about our human frailty and denial regarding disloyalty and betrayal for material gain.

Jefferson related to Jesus's admonition against violence, once saying, "I have the consolation to reflect that during the period of my administration not a drop of the blood of a single fellow citizen was shed by the sword of war or of the law." Jefferson believed war was irrational and evil, but he did authorize military force against the Barbary pirates.

The high priest then asked Jesus about his disciples and his doctrine. Jesus answered, I spoke openly to the world; I often taught in the synagogue, and in the temple where Jews congregate. I've said nothing in secret. Why do you ask me? ask those who heard me, what I said to them, they know what I said. When Jesus had spoken, a nearby officer struck Jesus with the palm of his hand saying, you answer the high priest this way? Jesus responded, If I have spoken evil, bear witness to that evil, but if I spoke well, why have you struck me? (J. 18:19-23) And they led Jesus away to the high priest: and with him were assembled all the chief priests, the elders, and the scribes. And the chief priests and all the council sought witnesses against Jesus to put him to death; and found none. For many bore false witness against him, but the witnesses did not agree. Some said they heard Jesus say, I will destroy this temple that is made with hands and within three days, I will build another without hands. But the witnesses did not agree. And the high priest stood up among them and asked Jesus, do you not answer what these witnesses say against you? Jesus held his peace and answered nothing. And again, the high priest asked him, are you the Christ, the Son of the Blessed? (Mk. 14:53, 55-61) And Jesus answered, if I tell you, you will not believe: and if I also ask you, you will not answer me, nor let me go. Then they all asked, are you the Son of God? And Jesus answered, you say that I am. (Lk. 22:67-68, 70) Then the high priest tore at his clothes and said, do we need further witnesses? You have heard the blasphemy: what do you think? And they all condemned him to be guilty of death. And some began to spit on him, to cover his face, and to buffet him, and to say to him, prophesy: and the servants struck him with the palms of their hands. (Mk. 14:63-65; also Mt.)

Only John narrates Jesus's questioning by the high priest's father-in-law Annas. But Mark, Matthew, and Luke report Jesus's interrogation by high priest Caiaphas and Jewish religious leaders threatened by his disturbance in the temple, his criticism of Pharisee hypocrisy, and his challenge to their authority. They saw him as a rabble-rouser and troublemaker, and as he was becoming more effective and influential, he had to go. Jesus failed in his immediate attempt to cure the ills of Judaism but succeeded in conveying his message of love and forgiveness.

Jefferson, perhaps seeing Jesus as an example, helped protest the abusive British rule and, somewhat like Jesus, upended the political order and helped foment the successful Revolutionary War.

Then they led Jesus from Caiaphas to the hall of judgment, and it was early, and the Jews themselves didn't go into the judgment hall, lest they be defiled; and not be able to eat the Passover meal. Pilate then went out to them and said, what accusation do you bring against this man? They answered and said, if he were not a malefactor, we would not have delivered him to you. Then Pilate said take him and judge him according to your law. The Jews said to him, Pilate it is not lawful for us to put a man to death. Then Pilate entered the judgment hall again, called Jesus and said to him, are you the King of the Jews? Jesus answered, do you say this thing yourself or did others tell you of this of me? Pilate answered, am I a Jew? your own nation and the chief priest have delivered you to me: what have you done? Jesus answered, my kingdom is not of this world. If my kingdom was of this world, then would my servants fight that I should not be delivered to the Jews. But now my kingdom is not from here. Pilate then said to him, are you a king? Jesus answered, you say that I am king. To this end I was born, and for this cause I came into the world, that I should bear witness to the truth. Everyone that is of the truth hears my voice. Pilate said, what is truth? And when he had said this, again he went out to the Jews and said to them, I find no fault in him at all. (J. 18:28-31, 33-38) And the Jews were more fierce saying, he stirs up the people, teaching throughout all Jewry, from Galilee to this place. (Lk. 23:5) Then Pilate said to him, do you hear how many things they accuse you of? (Mt. 27:13) When Pilate heard of Galilee, he asked whether the man was a Galilean? As soon as he knew that he belonged to Herod's jurisdiction, he sent him to Herod who himself was at Jerusalem at that time. And when Herod saw Jesus, he was glad: for he wanted to see him for a long time, because he had heard many things of him; and he hoped to see some miracle done by him. Then he questioned Jesus in many words, but Jesus answered nothing. And the chief priests and scribes stood and vehemently accused him. And Herod, with his men of war, set him and mocked him, and arrayed him in a gorgeous robe and send him back again to Pilate. And that same day Pilate and Herod were friends together for they had been enemies. And Pilate, when he had called together the chief priests and rulers of the people, said to them, you brought this man to me as one who perverted the people. I have examined him before you and found no fault of those things you have accused him. Nor has Herod: for I sent you to him, and nothing worthy of death has been found of Jesus. I will therefore chastise him and release him. (Lk. 23:6-16; also Mk.)

Jewish religious leaders either could not or would not condemn Jesus to death, which could only be done by the Roman occupying authority, Pontius Pilate. Rome generally tolerated alternate religions so long as they didn't upset or threaten their political order. The Pharisees may have convinced the Roman authorities that Jesus was a threat to civic order. Pilate, by John's account, expressed doubt but demurred and sent Jesus to Herod, the local Roman authority who also demurred and sent him back to Pilate. John, as a later gospel writer, deifies Jesus, having him say, "My

kingdom is not of this world," and furthers the concept of a spiritual rather than an earthly afterlife. He calls out legalistic and ritual Jewish practices, the fear of being unclean or of being barred from Passover. John tells of the acquiescence of the Romans, but primarily focuses blame on the Jews for Jesus's death.

Jefferson, not a believer in Jesus's deity, would have likely accepted only the story of the Roman conviction and execution of Jesus for his purported treasonous claim to be the King of the Jews.

Now, at that feast time, the governor by custom, released a prisoner of the people's choice and a notable prisoner was Barabbas. When they were gathered, Pilate said, whom should I release to you? Barabbas or Jesus who is called Christ? For he knew it was from envy that they had delivered Jesus. When Pilate sat on the judgment seat, his wife sent to him saying, have nothing to do with Jesus: for I have suffered many things this day in a dream because of him. But the chief priest and elders persuaded the multitude to ask for Barabbas and destroy Jesus. Pilate asked, which of the two should I release to you? They said Barabbas. Pilate said, then what should I do with Jesus who is called Christ? They all said, let him be crucified. And the governor said, why, what evil has he done? but they cried out more saying, let him be crucified. (Mt. 27:15-23) Then he released Barabbas to them: and when he had scourged Jesus, he delivered him to be crucified. Then the soldiers of the governor took Jesus into the common hall and a whole band of soldiers gathered around him. They wove a crown of thorns, placed it on his head, and put a reed in his right hand: and they bowed before him and mocked him saying, hail, king of the Jews! And they spit on him and took the reed and hit him on the head. And after they mocked him, they took off his robe, put on his own clothes and led him away to crucify him. (Mt. 27:26-27, 29-31) Then Judas, who had betrayed him, when he saw that he was condemned, repented. and brought the thirty pieces of silver to the chief priests and elders, saying, I have sinned in that I have betrayed an innocent blood. And they said, what is that to us? See you to that. And he cast down the pieces of silver in the temple and departed and went and hanged himself. And the chief priests took the silver pieces, and said, it is not lawful for us to put them in the treasury, because it is the price of blood. And they took counsel and bought with them a potter's field that was called the field of blood even to this day. (Mt. 27:3-8; also Mk., Lk., and J.)

The gospel writers described Jesus as a threat to the Jewish Pharisees, scribes, and priests and to the civic order, which legally required worship of the Roman emperor. Therefore, he was condemned and sentenced to death for treason as a common criminal, with Matthew and then

John ascribing most blame to the Jews. There were no known witnesses and so details of his trial, the scourging by soldiers, and the betrayal by Judas are all details imagined years after the facts.

Jefferson likely saw Jesus as an extraordinary *man* attempting to reform the established religious order but vilified by those in power, and that he suffered the ultimate personal sacrifice: crucifixion as a common criminal.

And as led him way, they laid hold of one Simon a Cyrenian coming out of the country, and on him they laid the cross that he might bare it after Jesus. And there followed him a great company of people and of women who also bewailed and lamented him. But Jesus turning to them said, daughters of Jerusalem weep not for me but weep for yourselves and for your children. For the days are coming in which they shall say, blessed are the barren and the wombs that never bear, and the paps that never gave suck. Then they shall begin to say to the mountains, fall on us; and to the hills, cover us. For if they do these things in a green tree, what shall be done in the dry? And there were two other malefactors led with him to also be put to death. (Lk. 23:26-32) And he, bearing his cross, went to a place called the place of a skull, which is called in the Hebrew, Golgotha: where they crucified him, and two others with him on either side and Jesus in the middle. And Pilate wrote a title and put it on the cross. And the writing was JESUS OF NAZARETH KING OF THE JEWS. This title was read by many of the Jews for the place where Jesus was crucified was near to the city, and it was written in Hebrew, Greek, and Latin. Then the chief priests of the Jews said to Pilate: write not The King of the Jews, but that he said, I am king of the Jews. Pilate answered, what I have written I have written. Then the soldiers, when they had crucified Jesus, took his garments, and made four parts, to every soldier was given a part; and also, his coat: now the coat was without seam, woven from the top throughout. They said therefore among themselves, let's not tear it, but cast lots for whose it shall be. (J. 19:17-24) And they who passed by reviled him, wagging their heads, and saying, you who destroyed the temple and built it in three days, save yourself. If you be the Son of God, come down from the cross. Likewise, the chief priests mocked him, with the scribes and elders said, he saved others; himself he cannot save. If he be the King of Israel, let him now come down from the cross, and we will believe him. He trusted in God; let him deliver him now, if he will have him: for he said, I am the Son of God. (Mt. 27:39-43) And one of the malefactors who was hanged railed on him saying, if are the Christ, save yourself and us. But the other answering rebuked him, saying do you not fear God, seeing you are in the same condemnation? And we are indeed justly; for we received the due reward of our deeds; but this man has done nothing amiss.

Then Jesus said, Father forgive them; for they know not what they do. (Lk. 23:39-41, 34) Now there stood by the cross of Jesus his mother, and his mother's sister, Mary, the wife of Cleophas, and Mary Magdalene. When Jesus saw his mother and the disciple standing by, whom he loved, he said to his mother, woman behold your Son! Then he said to his disciple, behold your mother! And from that hour that disciple took her into his own home. (J. 19:25-27) And about ninth hour, Jesus cried with a loud voice, ...My God, My God, why have you forsaken me? Some that stood there when they heard that, said, this man calls for Elijah. And straightaway, one of them ran, and took a sponge, and filled it with vinegar, and put it on a reed, and gave it to him to drink. The rest said, Let be, let us see if Elijah will come to save him. Jesus, when he had cried again with a loud voice, yielded up the ghost. Many women were there beholding from afar, who had followed Jesus from Galilee, ministering to him. Among them was Mary Magdalene, and Mary mother of James and Joses, and the mother of Zebedee's children. (Mt. 27:46-49, 50, 55, 56) The Jews, because it was the preparation, that the bodies should not remain on the cross on the sabbath day, (for that sabbath day was a high day,) asked Pilate that their legs might be broken, and that they might be taken away. The soldiers then came and broke the legs of the first and of the other who was crucified with him. But when they came to Jesus and saw that he was already dead, they did not break his legs: but one of the soldiers with his spear pierced his side, and out came blood and water. And after this Joseph of Arimathea (being a disciple of Jesus, but secretly for fear of the Jews,) asked Pilate that he might take away the body of Jesus: and Pilate gave him leave. He came therefore and took the body of Jesus. And Nicodemus also came (at first, he came to Jesus by night) and brought a mixture of myrrh and aloes, about a hundred-pound weight. Then they took the body of Jesus and wound it in linen cloth with the spices, as the manner of the Jews is to bury. Now, in that place where he was crucified, there was a garden; and in the garden a new sepulcher, where never a man yet laid. There they laid Jesus. (J. 19: 31-34, 38-42) And rolled a great stone to the door of the sepulcher and departed. (Mt. 27:60; also Mk.)

This description of the death and disposition of Jesus's body, with no known witnesses, was primarily created by gospel writer John, long after Jesus's death. Mark recounts Jesus, abandoned by the disciples, as buried in a rock tomb by a sympathetic member of the Jewish council. Later, John has the women who followed Jesus come on Sunday morning to the tomb, where they find it empty and are told by a young man in a white robe to go and tell the others that Jesus has risen and has gone before them to Galilee, "but they said nothing to anyone, for they were afraid" (Mk. 16:4-8). Some 25 years after Jesus's death, Mark likely relayed the common wisdom of the time,

attempting to reconcile what his disciples thought: that a great holy man had been crucified as a common criminal. They reasoned that resurrection must have always been part of the plan. The gospel of Mark, likely more historically accurate, ended with the women fleeing in fear from the empty tomb. The majority of recent scholars believe this to be the original, earliest, and most reliable manuscript.

Someone later added the following text to Mark's original gospel, and it was included in the King James Version bible. Because it included miracles and the resurrection, Jefferson excluded it: *Mk. 16:9 Now when Jesus was risen early the first day of the week, he appeared first to Mary Magdalene, out of whom he had cast seven devils. 10 And she went and told them that had been with him, as they mourned and wept. 11 And they, when they had heard that he was alive, and had been seen of her, believed not. 12 After that he appeared in another form unto two of them, as they walked, and went into the country. 13 And they went and told it unto the residue: neither believed they them. 14 Afterward he appeared unto the eleven as they sat at meat and upbraided them with their unbelief and hardness of heart, because they believed not them which had seen him after he was risen. 15 And he said unto them, Go ye into all the world, and preach the gospel to every creature. 16 He that believeth and is baptized shall be saved; but he that believeth not shall be damned. 17 And these signs shall follow them that believe; In my name shall they cast out devils; they shall speak with new tongues; 18 They shall take up serpents; and if they drink any deadly thing, it shall not hurt them; they shall lay hands on the sick, and they shall recover. 19 So then after the Lord had spoken unto them, he was received up into heaven, and sat on the right hand of God. 20 And they went forth, and preached everywhere, the Lord working with them, and confirming the word with signs following. Amen.*

The wrapping of Jesus and burial in a new sepulcher is unlikely. Those executed as criminals by the Romans were buried in a common grave.

Jefferson concluded *The Life and Morals of Jesus of Nazareth* **entries with the** *original* **Matthew burial passage. He excluded parallel resurrection passages by the other three evangelists.**

PART 5: PRAISE AND CRITICISM

"Whatever authority we may accept, it is we who accept it."

—Karl Raimund Popper

To create *The Life and Morals of Jesus of Nazareth*, Jefferson "cut and pasted" from six New Testament volumes in making his second compilation. He utilized (per monticello.org) two copies each of a 1794 Greek/Latin edition, a 1802 French edition, and a 1804 English edition. Did he circle back to the real words of his moral sage Jesus? The Enlightenment or Age of Reason had only just begun serious inquiry into the life and words of the historical Jesus, but ever-confident Jefferson may have seen his work as a complete and accurate representation of Jesus's life. And he further boldly predicted the end of so-called, revealed, literal, biblical truth. Jefferson had been called an atheist and spiritually unfit for office during his 1800 campaign for president. It's no wonder that he avoided pile-on controversy by not publishing (yet preserving) his Holy Bible handiwork.

Once discovered, and since its first official government publication in 1904 for members of Congress, *The Life and Morals of Jesus of Nazareth* was met with and still meets with much orthodox Christian scorn as an attack on the Bible. Some criticism is vehement, personal, and even threatening. Some critics believe that *The Jefferson Bible* discounts and undermines their Holy Bible, a sacrosanct text that, to them, is directly inspired by God:

"Doctrinally, he's a heretic. He doesn't believe in Jesus' divinity or the miracles or many of the central tenets of orthodox Christianity. And yet, when you read Jefferson's Bible you come away with the sense that he is quite religious in his own way, quite spiritual in his own way." Steven Waldman, author of *Founding Faith*.

Garrett Ward Sheldon, author of *The Political Philosophy of Thomas Jefferson*, says that Jefferson, a brilliant, practical, scientific man, didn't understand and didn't get spirituality. Peter Carlson (5/15/2023) The Bible According to Thomas Jefferson. HistoryNet Retrieved from https://www.historynet.com/bible-according-thomas-jefferson/

"In Jefferson, there's a lack—I really think it's a learning disability—a lack of understanding about spirituality." Garrett Ward Sheldon, a professor of political science at the University of Virginia and author of The Political Philosophy of Thomas Jefferson.

Cari Haus, critical author of *The Reverse Jefferson Bible,* which contains those passages left out of Jefferson's version, warns that God may harshly judge Jefferson for tampering with the official Bible.

Dr. R. Albert Mohler Jr., theologian, minister, and president, Southern Baptist Theological Seminary, calls Jefferson's extracting of the "real" Jesus from the gospels evidence of his hubris and arrogance (akin to my "improving" the literary work of Thomas Jefferson?). True Christianity, he says, stands or falls on the truthfulness of the gospels and entire historical biblical text. He cites Paul saying that without the Resurrection Christians are a people to be pitied. https://albertmohler.com/2005/11/28/a-postmodernist-before-his-time-thomas-jefferson-on-jesus-2

In 2009, Israel Drazin claimed that *The Jefferson Bible* violated Jesus's basic teachings and had no relation to the New Testament. He said that Jefferson distorted what he intended to improve and created "an embarrassment to thinking and considerate people." Israel Drazin, 2009, http://www.historyinreview.org/tj_jefbible.html

John J. Miller, in an Angelus News book review, calls *The Jefferson Bible* "a heretical document" and "a deviation from the standards of Christian faith." To him, the gospels are a package deal, meaning that we can't pick and choose the passages to believe or disbelieve. He admits, though, that Jefferson's work has generated curiosity and admiration alongside disgust and denunciation. He concludes that, without the miracles, *The Jefferson Bible* is uninspiring and boring. https://angelusnews.com/arts-culture/an-american-presidents-heretical-bible/

Ed Simon commented on Peter Manseau's review of *The Jefferson Bible* that Jefferson eliminated from the original gospels "every single interesting thing about Jesus," cutting the virgin birth, the miracle of water into wine, and the raising

Lazarus from dead. https://lareviewofbooks.org/article/doubting-thomas-on-peter-manseaus-the-jefferson-bible/

However, some seemed ambivalent:

"Religion for many fills a spiritual requirement. Faith can compel marvelous deeds, can help someone push through relentless adversity. Where would Martin Luther King, Jr., have been without it? And where would America be without King?" WayneLaufert:https://thehumanist.com/magazine//features/vonnegut-and-jefferson-and-jesus/ 14 June 2022

"Why did one of America's beloved Founding Fathers cut up Bibles? Was it an act of piety or of blasphemy? Was Jefferson a Christian or a heretic? And what does this book, commonly known as the 'Jefferson Bible,' tell us about America's religious heritage? ...one thing seems certain: If Jefferson was running for president today, his Bible-slicing experiments would surely torpedo his candidacy." The Bible According to Thomas Jefferson, by PeterCarlson,https://thehumanist.com/magazine/march-april-2012/features/the-bible-according-to-thomas-jefferson/

David Felten, pastor of the Fountains United Methodist Church in an April 13, 2023, essay, says that the Bible itself is totally the problem, calling Paul's epistle efforts a "train wreck. Jesus didn't die in some cosmic pay-off to an angry God oranthropomorphic Satan. He died as a result of...fearful, unjust, oppressive, and insecure human beings."

https://progressingspirit.com/2023/04/13/retiring-atonement-preferably-with-extreme-prejudice

Others appreciated and supported Jefferson's bold work:

"Jefferson did (his bible) in a somewhat audacious way, but I think it's also respectful. He's not trashing Jesus. He's writing to his colleagues saying this is the greatest moral teacher of all time, and these moral principles can be the basis for the new republic." Harry Rubenstein, Smithsonian curator worked on the Bible.

https://americanhistory.si.edu/about/departments/political-and-military-history

"As with many Unitarians of like spirit who had followed him, Jefferson's was a search for the intelligible Jesus. Jesus was, eloquent, benevolent, innocent, a victim first of the Roman state and then of the Christian church."

Forrest Church is a senior minister of All Souls Church, NY and author of *Lifecraft*.

Kilgore Trout in *Slaughterhouse-Five*, in a passage that exhibits Jeffersonian Christianity, exalts Jesus—or at least his teachings—while purposefully stripping away his divinity, and:

Trout's *Gospel from Outer Space* is about an alien who visits Earth and studies Christianity to find out "why Christians found it so easy to be cruel." In part, the alien concludes, the problem is "slipshod storytelling in the New Testament."-Kurt Vonnegut: https://thehumanist.com/magazine//features/vonnegut-and-jefferson-and-jesus/ 14 June 2022

Jefferson wasn't the first or only person to show Jesus as human, not divine. Biblical Scholar Bart Ehrman points to early Bible texts referring to Joseph and Mary as Jesus's parents, and to where later edits or corrections that altered the text to make Jesus the Son of God and born of a virgin. Ehrman, Bart D., Misquoting Jesus, 2005, HarperCollins

Dr. Carl Krieg, in a Progressive Christianity article from November 10, 2022, says that the New Testament reveals an astounding contrast between "what Jesus taught, on the one hand, and what the later first-century writers taught, on the other. What we find is basically a transition from a transformative and prophetic movement to a reactionary religious organization that lives on with us even today." *The Birth and Death of the Church in the First Century - Part 1*-https://mailchi.mp/a901e6a35a7a/the-birth-and-death-of-the-church-in-the-first-century-part-1?e=fc857259f2

Steve Waldman (again), in 2019, thought Jefferson focused on preserving freedom and aimed to diminish the controlling threat posed by modern and ancient organized religion. Jefferson remained pro Jesus but turned against blind faith and organizational Christianity- https://www.nationalreview.com/2019/05/james-madison-understood-religious-freedom-better-than-jefferson-did/

In his review of *The Jefferson Bible* for *The Wall Street Journal*, published on September 30, 2022, Crawford Gribben writes: "Jefferson kept his project secret, worried that his freethinking devotional pastime could become a serious political liability and discussed it with only a handful of similarly enlightened friends. He had little to be worried about. The nation that he and his philosophical friends created in their image needed this version of Jesus."- https://www.wsj.com/articles/the-jefferson-bible-review-the-gospel-sans-miracles-11601507322

Published praise for *The Jefferson Bible: The Life and Morals of Jesus of Nazareth*-Publisher: Beacon Press, July 4, 2001.

"Religion in America [gained] something unique from Jefferson...His Jesus was a figure fitted for the Enlightenment, rational but not divine." — Gustav Niebuhr, *New York Times*

"The Founding Father's treatment of the Bible was radical.... Today, historians such as Yale University's Jaroslav Pelikan are struck by the project's 'sheer audacity'...Jefferson's Bible is a curious sidelight on an ever-intriguing figure, whose image has become more controversial in recent years." — Richard N. Ostling, Associated Press

[The Jefferson Bible] "Gives us a preaching Jesus of distinctly human dimensions, without miracles or resurrection. [A] fascinating document, telling us a great deal about a great eighteenth-century mind and its world." — Charles S. Adams, *Religious Studies Review*

"These excerpts from the four Gospels are among the most interesting and compelling in all of the Scripture. They emphasize Jesus' ethical lessons of love, reverence, forbearance, reproachment, repentance, and forgiveness." — Garrett Ward Sheldon (again), *Virginia Magazine of History and Biography*

General Related Comments:

John Shelby Spong, the late Episcopal bishop, like Jefferson, disbelieved that miracle, such as Jesus's virgin birth or his bodily resurrection, were added in the eighth and ninth centuries C.E. Spong says:

"Stones are not rolled away...dead bodies do not walk out of tombs three days after execution, people don't still storms, or walk on water." Jefferson knew and cut out these "mythological human attempts to use extraordinary language" to explain the disciples' experiences. Spong would have also supported Jefferson's excising of many biblical passages advocating bigotry, religious persecution, religious wars, and the Inquisition. John Shelby Spong, Sins of Scriptures, HarperCollins, 2005

Neither Jefferson nor, much later, Spong accepted the Bible's story of atonement, the prehistoric idea of a sacrifice to gods (mistakenly revived by Paul). Both thought that a focus on Jesus's death distorted his life's example of forgiveness and unconditional love.

> "Historical scholarship has amply demonstrated that holy scriptures are all-to-human products of their historical eras, including internal contradictions, factual errors, plagiarisms from neighboring civilizations and scientific absurdities…. The recondite arguments from sophisticated theologians are no sounder." Steven Pinker, Enlightenment Now, 2018, Penguin Random House

Was Jefferson the Bible critic the odd man out among his fellow founding fathers? Well, he had been most vehement regarding the separation of church and state and perhaps the only to commit his Bible criticism to extensive writing. But many cohorts were of a similar mind. For one, Jefferson's approach was supported by his frenemy John Adams:

> "The divinity of Jesus is made a convenient cover for absurdity. Nowhere in the Gospels do we find a precept for Creeds, Confessions, Oaths, Doctrines, and whole cartloads of other foolish trumpery that we find in Christianity." and,

> "The question before the human race is, whether the God of Nature shall govern the world by his own laws, or whether priests and kings shall rule it by fictitious miracles?"

Many fellow Deists were among the founding fathers, including Jefferson's much senior colleague Ben Franklin, who was a proponent of generic religion but not a practitioner. He prayed to "Powerful Goodness" and referred to God as "the infinite." Franklin considered Jesus's system of morals to be the best that the world had ever seen or is likely to ever see but regretted its "various corrupt changes," and doubted Jesus's divinity.

Fellow founder and Deist Thomas Paine had similar views but was more outspoken. In his famous *The Age of Reason*, he called Christianity "little more than the idolatry of the ancient mythologists." Called "an end-of-century throwback to Thomas Chubb" in Charlotte Allen's *The Human Christ*, Paine publicly called the Bible and New Testament "impositions on the world"; deemed the belief in the fall of man, Jesus Christ as the Son of God dying to appease sins against God, and seeking salvation as unworthy of the "wisdom and power of the Almighty"; as well as stated that the only true religion is the belief of one God and the practice of moral virtues.

Paine, like Jefferson, discounted the revelation of the Bible but thought the *real* Jesus a moral, virtuous, and admirable man. On revelation, Paine thought that if someone did hear the voice of God, "When he tells it to a second person" and that person tells it to others, "it is revelation to that (first) person only and hearsay to every other; and consequently, they are not obligated to believe it." Jennifer Michael Hecht, Doubt, p. 356

Many founding fathers were Deist, but many more were ostensibly and actually Christian, resulting in Thomas Jefferson, our third president, warily sharing his Bible views with only a few of his cohorts, as in his late-in-life letter to John Adams: "[T]he truth is that the greatest enemies to the doctrines of Jesus (the expositors) who have perverted them for...a system of fancy absolutely incomprehensible, and without any foundation in his genuine words." Monticello.org: 1823 April 11

Part 6: Conclusion

Why did Jefferson write *The Life and Morals of Jesus of Nazareth—The Jefferson Bible*? And what does it mean to us today?

Jefferson knew the abuses of the Hebrew Pharisees and scribes related directly to their appointment, collaboration, and as such control by their Roman occupiers. Once they became state-sponsored, Jewish religious leaders stayed in power and sustained systemic privilege by answering to Herod Antipas (reign: 4 B.C.E. – 39 C.E.) rather than to their Hebrew scriptures. Jesus targeted them and their Roman overlords for reform, resulting in his death and the subsequent socially and politically influenced recordings of those events in the gospels.

Jefferson, an Enlightenment activist and acclaimed writer, chaffed at what he saw as the resulting false and distorted history of the man Jesus. He felt compelled to right the record—and not incidentally to object to the church/government institutional control stemming from that traditional Christian Bible.

Realizing that no one can be "created equal" unless they're free to decide their conscience on religious beliefs, he helped de-Christianize Virginia and the U.S. Constitution and de-Anglicize the University of Virginia. He foresaw that battle to be ongoing, and to leave no doubt as to the central importance of maintaining separation of church and state to all other freedoms, he boldly exercised that right by creating his own not-church-or-state-sanctioned Bible.

As a humanist, a son of the Enlightenment, and pluralist, Jefferson advocated for religious freedom for "the Jew and the Gentile, the Christian and Mahometan, the Hindoo, the infidel of every denomination." Jefferson knew throughout history that state and religion repeatedly combined forces, leading to a toxic authoritarianism that left neither institution useful nor free.

Jefferson anticipated that the church and state would forever be drawn toward unholy autocratic rule, precluding the enlightened self-interest of either. *The Jefferson Bible* wasn't only about his disagreement about the historical Jesus, but also became his "a sect by myself" final testament to his religious beliefs and everyone's right to believe, or not, free from state control. Exercising his right to write heresy and rewrite biblical history became his final declaration of independence—his personal revolution against the forces of the political and religious establishment.

So what? You were thinking that his Bible would be a poke in the eye to his hypocritical political tormentors throughout his elected career? Well, maybe it was that too.

What meaning does *The Jefferson Bible* have for us today?

To some, Jefferson's cut-and-paste version of the Bible is held up as evidence that America is a Christian nation based on the gospels. Others see the founding fathers' intent in the Constitution as rooting out any influence of faith or control of institutional religion.

According to Forrest Church in *The Separation of Church and State*, founding fathers Thomas Jefferson and

James Madison aimed to secure the republic and its citizens from the "spiritual tyranny" of any and every religion. Their Enlightenment values called for freedom *from* the dictates of any and all organized religions. Those supporting those views included John Adams, John Jay, and Alexander Hamilton. President George Washington also affirmed his sworn fidelity to state-church separation, and in 1797 so did the entire U.S. Senate when they ratified the Treaty of Tripoli.

* * *

Thomas Jefferson and James Madison could never have imagined that their 18th-century opponents' arguments would survive until today. They'd be pleased that, per a 2021 Pew poll, that almost 70 percent of U.S. respondents say that the government should never declare any official religion. But they'd be aghast that *nearly 20 percent* of those respondents say that the federal government should stop enforcing the separation of church and state, and that *15 percent* say that the federal government should declare the U.S. a Christian nation (based, of course, on their *real* Bible)

But today's echo of "freedom of religion," has been distorted by far-right conservatives, and is being used to recombine church and state by fostering Christianity as a new at least state-preferred religion. Many of these conservatives politically argue, and falsely so, that we began as a Christian nation and that our republic will only survive by adhering to Judeo-Christian principles. They maintain that nothing in the Virginia statute or Bill of Rights excludes state intrusion in religious matters if state intrusion is neutral or non-preferential. But they are wrong.

They forget or ignore that Jefferson precisely rejected that rationale in Virginia, saying that it is "sinful and tyrannical" to compel a person to support opinions that he doesn't share and went on to declare that even "forcing him to support this or that teacher of his own religious persuasions" is wrong, and isn't liberty at all. That sounds a bit like vouchers for Christian or other sectarian schools, no?

Jefferson also famously said in his Notes on the State of Virginia, which were written in 1781 and somewhat corrected and enlarged in 1782, "The legitimate powers of government extend to such acts only as are injurious to others. But it does me no injury for my neighbor to say there are twenty gods, or no god. It neither picks my pocket nor breaks my leg."

On October 7, 1822, Jefferson spoke more emphatically to the University of Virginia about this matter: "...(T)he constitutional freedom of religion [is] the most inalienable and sacred of all rights."

*　*　*

Katherine Stewart in *The Power Worshippers* refers to "freedom of religion" conservatives and Christian nationalists:

"This kind of 'liberty' is really just a form of religious privilege. This new religious right—a license to discriminate—has become one of the chief talking points of leaders of the Christian nationalist movement, which ties the idea of America to specific religious and cultural identities....a partisan appeal to conservative religious voters....Christian nationalism looks backward on a fictionalized history of

America's allegedly Christian founding….pretend(ing)…the revival of 'traditional values' yet…contradicts the long-established principles and norms of our democracy. It is a political movement, and its ultimate goal is power. It (seeks) to replace our foundational democratic principles (with) a particular version of Christianity…a 'biblical worldview'…(that) now determines the future of the Republican Party. (To) defend against Christian nationalists' distorted notion of 'religious liberty,'…we just need to reclaim the genuine religious freedom that our founders established and that most of our citizens cherish. (We need) …to undermine the pretensions of those who would dominate us in the name of God."

Current threats exist even within our courts. Merrill D. Peterson, in his December 1994 article "Thomas Jefferson and Religious Freedom" for *The Atlantic Monthly*, notes our precious legacy of church and state separation but warns of even the U.S. Supreme Court's danger to freedom of religion rights by their challenging of the Religious Freedom Restoration Act (RFRA), Congress's attempt to restore former standards of state nonintervention in religious practices.

Threats exist in so-called red states: In 2018, per research.lifeway.com, the Commercial Appeal reported that, according to Tennessee law, "in order to solemnize the rite of marriage, any such minister, preacher, pastor, priest, rabbi or other spiritual leader must be ordained or otherwise designated in conformity with the customs of a church, temple or other religious group or organization; and such customs must provide for such ordination or designation by a considered, deliberate, and responsible act."

Even in so-called blue states, leaders aren't always supportive of church and state separation: On February 2, 2023, *The New York Times* reported that at the annual interfaith breakfast, New York City Mayor Eric Adams said, "Don't tell me about no separation of church and state. State is the body. Church is the heart. You take the heart out of the body, the body dies." He added, "When we took prayers out of schools, guns came into schools."

But Nicole Penn, per her article "Thomas Jefferson's Not-So-Peculiar Mind" for *The Bulwark,* firmly supports and appreciates Jefferson's wall of separation: "It is indisputable that one of the greatest gifts Jefferson left this country was to decouple religion from political power; to give every woman and man the opportunity to form their own consciences without the direction of the heavy hand of the state."

President Joe Biden adds his support (www.state.gov/reports/2020-report-on-international-religious-freedom/): "The work of protecting religious freedom, for people of all faiths and none, is never finished….(We) will guard these cherished principles, working shoulder-to-shoulder with Americans of all beliefs to preserve our nation's founding promise as an enduring citadel of diversity, unity, and mutual respect."

Jefferson predicted the growth of religious diversity, suggesting that freedom from government would benefit all varieties of religious experience. So far, his ideas about individual freedom have prevailed in the form of pluralism and variations of religions, since many today have decided their own spiritual way; there are an estimated 2,200 distinct religious groups and denominations currently in the United States. According to Pew polling, the fastest-growing segment of Americans are those who say they have no religious faith or identify themselves as atheists, agnostics, or humanists.

* * *

Thomas Jefferson subscribed to the Christian ethics of equality, toleration, and freedom of conscience as *natural* rights and rejected religion's claims of inequality between believers and unbelievers and intolerance of the latter as somehow willed by God. He believed that we can all be inspired by faith, tradition, and great human examples, yet always we must decide our own spiritual path (or not). Jefferson asked us to accept here-on-earth personal responsibility for our enlightened best interests—based on reason, not on religious afterlife reward or punishment. He called his religious views private, *but* he bound his Bible in red leather, passed it to his family, and likely intended it to reinforce everybody's right to interpret and decide their own god and personal religion, unencumbered by state control or influence. He foresaw that institutional Christianity would never give up control if combined with the power of the state. Without that wall of separation, his and all others' personal spirituality and beliefs about Jesus or, especially, opinions contrary to state-sanctioned religion would be quashed.

Jefferson saw the Jesus of history as a Judean folk philosopher, a radical religious reformer, and a teacher of enlightened morality. It seemed to him that to glorify their hero Jesus, evangelists Mark, Mathew, Luke, and John mirrored the early church in creating an object to praise and worship with little resemblance to the historical itinerant preacher of Nazareth. Jefferson would likely today agree with Elaine Pagels, who states in *The Gnostic Gospels* that Jesus's miracle resurrection served a political function by legitimizing exclusive leadership authority for Peter, the 11 loyal apostles, and their anointed successor bishops and future clerical chains of command. Yet Jefferson knew that without the guarantee of freedom of religion, a Christian hierarchy could become the only accepted authority.

Did Jefferson intend us to accept his Bible as our own spiritual/religious belief? I don't think so. Those passages that he chose, along with those that he rejected, were personal to him. I believe that he deliberately flaunted the then-established effective, state-approved Bible and religious order to exercise his personal freedom of religion. He never intended for his Bible to be *our* Bible.

A dear best friend pointed out that, "We all listen to different music." I can't argue for Jefferson's rationality as the only approach. Many believe in the miracles of the Bible and the divinity of Jesus. As Pope Francis said about gays, who am I to judge? Many believe in the miracle of life on this planet and of a supreme, not-human-knowable force of ongoing creation. And aren't the exquisite plans of evolution and the laws of physics a "miracle"?

We can all support the comfort and peace that the Bible provides for believers, especially at the time of the death of a loved one—comfort that I suspect Jefferson felt on the death of his beloved wife. And how about the miracle of courage and sacrifice of Jesus, who stood up to the corrupt religious and political authorities of his day, knowing the fatal consequences?

Jefferson made two points: We're each entitled to our personal spiritual beliefs, and to protect that right we need to guard and support true separation of church and state.

There is another land we've been conjuring upon which we might build a peaceful future. Formed of the same elements of our early dreams, the hopes we pasted on the heavens, it began to coalesce as we lifted ourselves, theory by theory, truth by truth, out of the murk of childhood's unknowing and into the accessibility of shared knowledge, out of the chaos of ignorance and into the promise of reason, out of absolute truths and into unceasing wonder….it has steadily been realized over the past centuries. It writes a different

future…. It is the land we create beyond the beliefs that divide.

From an essay by Rev. Gretta Vosper, June 1, 2023, Progressing Spirit

Appendix A. Gospel of Thomas

A. Gospel of Thomas: Excerpts included here show the commonality between and, perhaps, some of the origins of the gospels of Mark, Matthew, Luke, and John.

According to the Jesus Seminar, the sayings below are actually or probably spoken by Jesus and are also included in various forms in the four gospels quoted by Jefferson.

Quoted text in *italics:* comments in **bold.**

"These are the secret sayings that the living Jesus spoke, and Didymos Judas Thomas recorded."

2. Jesus said, *"Those who seek should not stop seeking until they find. For there is nothing hidden that will not be revealed."*

9. Jesus said, *"Look, the sower (farmer) went out, took a handful of seeds and scattered them some fell on the road and the birds came and gathered them others fell on rock and they didn't take root in the soil and didn't produce heads of green others fell on thorns, and they choked the seeds and worms ate them and others fell on good soil and it produced a good crop it yielded 60 per measure and 120 per measure."*

Some will hear the words of Jesus and repent. Many will hear but not change their ways.

10. Jesus said, *"I have cast fire upon the world, and look, I'm guarding it until it blazes."*

I bring light to the world and keep it lit.

14. Instructing his apostles, Jesus said, *"When you go into any region and walk about in the countryside, when people take you in, eat what they serve you…. After all, what goes into your mouth will not defile you; rather, it's what comes out of your mouth that will defile you."* **Adapt to your environment. No need to worry about Jewish dietary laws and other religious practices.**

20. And, to Jesus's disciples: *"It's like a mustard seed. It's the smallest of all seeds, but when it falls on prepared soil, it produces a large plant and becomes shelter for the birds of the sky."* **Metaphor for heaven's imperial rule. For Jesus, God's domain was to grow here on earth.**

26. Jesus said, *"You see the sliver in your friend's eye, but you don't see the timber in your own eye. When you take the timber out of your own eye, then you will see well enough to remove the sliver from your friend's eye."* **Forgive and see and correct your own faults before criticizing others.**

31. Jesus said, *"No prophet is welcome on his home turf."* **Jesus failed to gain acceptance in his own neighborhood.**

32. Jesus said, *"A city built on a high hill and fortified cannot fall, nor can it be hidden."* **Ancient cities were built on the mounds of prior city ruins. Jesus compared Christians to a**

city on a hill, meaning a beacon, providing spiritual light to the world.

33. Jesus said, *"After all, no one lights a lamp and puts it under a basket, nor does one put it in a hidden place. Rather, one puts it on the lamp stand so that all who come and go will see its light."* **Jesus's message of light is meant to be revealed, not concealed.**

36. Jesus said, *"Do not fret, from morning to evening and from evening to morning (about what to eat or wear) You're much better than the lilies, which neither card nor spin."* **Disregard concern for food or clothes except what is needed for the day.**

45. Jesus said, *"Grapes are not harvested from thorn trees, nor are figs gathered from thistles."* **Good comes from good people, evil from bad people.**

47. Jesus said, *"And a slave cannot serve two masters, otherwise that slave will honor the one and offend the other."* **Don't become a slave to money rather than God.**

"Nobody drinks aged wine and immediately wants to drink young wine. Young wine is not poured into old wineskins, or they might break, and aged wine is not poured into new wineskin, or it might spoil." **Jesus pits his own, new way against the old way of Hebrew religious leaders.**

54. Jesus said, *"Congratulations to the poor, for to you belongs heaven's domain."* **Jesus focused his message on the poor and dispossessed.**

62. Jesus said, *"Do not let your left hand know what your right hand is doing."* **Be modest and keep your charity giving secret.**

63. Jesus said, *"There was a rich person who had a great deal of money. He said, 'I shall invest my money so that I may sow, reap, plant, and fill my store houses with produce, that I may lack nothing.' These were the things he was thinking in his heart, but that very night he died."* **Jesus warns that life isn't about material possessions, and you can't take it with you.**

64. Jesus said, *"A person was receiving guests...."* (See Luke 14:16-24). **Many are called but few are chosen; the poor are favored over the wealthy.**

65. He said, *"A person owned a vineyard and rented it to some farmers, so they could work it and he could collect its crop from them. He sent his slave so the farmers would give him the vineyards crop. They grabbed him, beat him, and almost killed him and the slave returned and told his master. His master said, 'Perhaps he didn't know them.' He sent another slave and the farmers beat that one as well. Then the master sent his son and said, 'Perhaps they'll show my son some respect.' Because the farmers knew that he was the heir to the vineyard, they grabbed him and killed him."* **The story of how God's original favor was transferred from the non-accepting Jews to the Christians.**

78. Jesus said, *"Why have you come out to the countryside? To see a reed shaken by the wind? And to see a person dressed in soft clothes [like your rulers] and your powerful ones?"* **Being attached to comfort leads you away from being spiritual.**

86. Jesus said, *"Foxes have their dens and birds have their nests, but humans have no place to rest."* **Jesus warns his followers to expect to be poor and even homeless like him.**

89. Jesus said, *"Why do you wash the outside of the cup question don't you understand that the one who made the inside is also the one who made the outside?"* **This is a critique of the Jewish ritual of washing of utensils and vessels, rather than a focus on basic human values.**

95. Jesus said, *"If you have money, don't lend it at interest. Rather, give it to someone from whom you won't get it back."* **This is Jesus advocating for the poor.**

96. Jesus said, *"The Father's imperial rule is like a woman [who put a little leaven] in dough and made it into a large loaf of bread."* **This concerns the leverage effect of good deeds, with Jesus encouraging his disciples to spread his message.**

99. When told of his mother and brothers standing outside, Jesus said, *"Those here who do what my Father wants are my brothers and my mother."* **The outsiders are the Jews who reject him, and his family are the accepting gentiles.**

100. They showed Jesus a gold coin and said to him, *"The Roman emperor's people demand taxes from us."* He said to them, Give the Emperor what belongs to the emperor, give God what belongs to God." **Jesus avoids an attempt to trap him in treason to the Roman emperor.**

113. His disciples asked, "When will the Father's imperial rule come?" He said, *"It will not come by watching for it.... Rather, the Father's imperial rule is spread out upon the earth, and the people don't see it."*

And not Jesus Seminar but closely related:

3. *Jesus said, "If your leaders say to you, 'Look the kingdom is in heaven,' then the birds will precede you. Rather, the kingdom is inside you and it is outside you. When you come to know yourselves...then you will know that...you are the children of God."*

God's rule, the Kingdom of God, is already present on earth, and per Elaine Pagels's *The Gnostic Gospels*, self-knowledge is knowledge of God, as the self and the divine are identical.

B. Jefferson: Well, Nobody's Perfect

Thomas Jefferson famously declared us independent of royal and divine rule. He asked us to accept here-on-earth personal responsibility in our (Spinozan-) enlightened best interests—based on reason, not on religious afterlife reward or punishment.

Jefferson claimed of his Bible editing that he separated the diamond passages from those he considered dung. How did he do in his personal life? His all-men-created-equal and soaring human goals were diamonds. His intellectual and material life of luxury and personal privilege were enabled by the dung of maintaining enslaved humans.

On the issue of slavery his *heart* may have been in the right place, but perhaps not his **head:**

1764 age 21: Jefferson took charge of 30 inherited slaves.

1770 age 26: He defended a young mixed-race male slave in a freedom suit, on the grounds that his mother was white and freeborn.

1770 age 26: Began building Monticello with slave labor.

1772 age 28: Jefferson represented George Manly, the son of a free woman of color, who sued for freedom. Once freed, Manly worked for Jefferson at Monticello for wages.

1774 age 30: Wrote A Summary View of the Rights of British America: "The abolition of domestic slavery is the great object of desire in those colonies, where it was unhappily introduced in their infant state."

1776 age 32: Made a declaration and general criticism against slavery by maintaining that "all men are created equal."

1776 age 32: Submitted a draft for the new Virginia Constitution containing the phrase "No person hereafter coming into this country shall be held within the same in slavery under any pretext whatever."

1778 age 34: With his leadership and probable authorship, the Virginia General Assembly banned importing people to be used as slaves into Virginia.

1784 age 40: Submitted to the Continental Congress the "Report of a Plan of Government for the Western Territory," which would have prohibited slavery in all new states carved out of the western territories.

1786 age 42: "The voice of a single individual of the state, which was divided, or of one of those which were of the negative, would have prevented this abominable crime (slavery) from spreading itself over the new country."

1787 age 43: "The whole commerce between master and slave is a perpetual exercise of the most boisterous passions, the most unremitting despotism on the one part, and degrading submissions on the other." Also, he called slavery a moral evil for which the nation would ultimately have to account to God (Notes on the State of Virginia).

1787 age 43: Wrote of his "suspicion" that Black people were mentally and physically inferior to whites *but argued that they nonetheless had innate human rights.* **He therefore supported colonization plans that would transport freed slaves to another country.**

1787 to 1789: Negotiated with Sally Hemings in Paris to return to enslavement at Monticello in exchange for "extraordinary privileges" for herself and freedom for her unborn children. Decades later, Jefferson freed all Hemings's children.

https://www.monticello.org/thomas-jefferson/jefferson-slavery/thomas-jefferson-and-sally-hemings-a-brief-account/

1791 age 47: In a letter to Benjamin Banneker, dated August 30, 1791, he wrote: "Nobody wishes more than I do to see such proofs as you exhibit, that nature has given to our black brethren, talents equal to those of the other colors of men, and that the appearance of a want of them is owing merely to the degraded condition of their existence."

1792 age 48: In a letter to George Washington, he wrote: "Birth of black children [into his slavery] yielded a 4% annual profit."

1794 age 50: Started an unhealthy, hot, smokey nailery using slave boys ages 10 to 16. *Industrious ones were trained and promoted to a higher-level artisan, butler, or manager,* **but they remained slaves.**

1794 age 50: Freed Robert Hemings.

1796 age 52: Used slaves as collateral for Monticello renovation loan.

1796 age 52: Freed James Hemings.

1801-1809: During his presidency, Jefferson, as he witnessed a dangerous rift between the North and the South resulting

from congressional debate, remained publicly silent on slavery and emancipation.

1804 age 60: Compromise supported a one-year ban on Louisiana slave-trafficking.

1805 age 61: In an 1805 letter to William A. Burwell, he wrote: "I have long since given up the expectation of any early provision for the extinguishment of slavery among us." And in the same year, in a letter to George Logan, he wrote: "I have most carefully avoided every public act or manifestation on that subject." Jefferson avoided touching the political "third rail" of his time.

1806 age 62: Proposed a law during his annual congressional message "to withdraw the citizens of the United States from all further participation in those violations of human rights...which the morality, the reputation, and the best interests of our country have long been eager to proscribe." He denounced the international slave trade as a "violation of human rights" and called upon Congress to criminalize it. Congress approved the Act Prohibiting Importation of Slaves in 1807. **However, the act didn't limit but rather increased the importance and value of the domestic slave trade.**

1810 age 66: Had runaway slave Hubbard captured and "...had him severely flogged...and committed to jail."

1814 age 70: "There is nothing I would not sacrifice to a practicable plan of abolishing every vestige of this moral and political depravity," Jefferson wrote to Thomas Cooper on September 10, 1814.

https://www.poplarforest.org/learn/thomas-jeffersons-life-and-times/the-enslaved-people-of-poplar-forest/jeffersons-views-on-slavery/

1817 age 73: Maintained at 140, his highest slave population at Monticello.

1819 age 75: Opposed Missouri Statehood Amendment that banned slave importation and freed male slaves at age 25. He thought it "would destroy the Union."

1820 age 76: "There is not a man on earth who would sacrifice more than I would, to relieve us from this heavy reproach [slavery]...we have the wolf by the ears, and we can neither hold him, nor safely let him go. Justice is in one scale, **and self-preservation in the other." Jefferson wrote that to John Holmes on the Missouri Compromise. He thought that his cherished federal union, the world's first democratic experiment, would be destroyed by the fight for and against slavery.**

1820 age 77: Jefferson cut and pasted his The Life and Morals of Jesus of Nazareth Extracted textually from the Gospels in Greek/Latin, French, and English, now known as The Jefferson Bible.

1826 age 83: Died on the Fourth of July—as did John Adams.

Thomas Jefferson *called slavery a "moral depravity" and a "hideous blot,"* **but continued to hold human beings as property for his entire adult life.**

1827–1830 Posthumous: *At his death, in his will, Jefferson freed five additional slaves, bringing the total to 10 from the same family.* **However, he was greatly in debt due to his** extravagant lifestyle and in part due to his continued Monticello slave-labor construction program. Those estate debts forced his family to sell 130 slaves, virtually all the members of every slave family from Monticello, to pay his creditors. Slave families who had been well established and stable for decades were sometimes split up. Some slaves remained in Virginia, but others were relocated to Ohio.

This section is partially adapted from: https://en.wikipedia.org/wiki/Thomas_Jefferson_and_slavery

C. What Jefferson Deleted

Some traditional Bible passages Jefferson saw as absurd, false, or delusional and were not included in his personal Bible. Here are some of Jefferson's discarded "dross," and most would now say that they aren't characteristic of the Jesus of love and forgiveness:

Matthew 10:34-37: *Think not that I am come to send peace on earth: I came not to send peace, but a sword. For I am come to set a man at variance against his father, and the daughter against her mother....*

Matthew 12:30-32: *He that is not with me is against me.*

Matthew 10:1: *And when he had called unto him his twelve disciples, he gave them power against unclean spirits, to cast them out, and to heal all manner of sickness and all manner of disease.*

Mark 16:15-18: *And he said unto them, Go ye into all the world, and preach the gospel to every creature. He that believeth and is baptized shall be saved; but he that believeth not shall be damned. And these signs shall follow them that believe; In my name shall they cast out devils; they shall speak with new tongues.*

Luke 12:51-53: *Suppose ye that I am come to give peace on earth? I tell you, Nay, but rather division:*

Luke 14:26 *If any man come to me, and hate not his father, and mother, and wife, and children, and brethren, and sisters, yea, and his own life also, he cannot be my disciple.*

John 6:53-55: *Then Jesus said unto them, Verily, verily, I say unto you, Except ye eat the flesh of the Son of man, and drink his blood, ye have no life in you.*

John 12:25: *He that loves his life shall lose it; and he that hates his life in this world shall keep it unto life eternal.*

A Jefferson Bible for the Twenty-first Century. Humanist Press LLC. Kindle Edition.

D. Much Credit, Many Thanks, and Recommended Reading:

Armstrong, Karen, *A History of God,* 1993, Ballantine Books

Aslan, Reza, *Zealot, The Life and Times of Jesus of Nazareth*, 2013, Random House

Bloom, Harold, *The Gospel of Thomas*, 1992, Harper Collins

Barton, John, *A History of the Bible*, 2020, Penguin Publishing Group. Kindle Edition.

Barton, John, www.latimes.com/opinion/story/2021-04-04/christians-heaven-hell-soul

Church, Forrest, Ed., *The Separation of Church and State*, 2004, Beacon Press

Dewey, Arthur, Et al., *The Authentic Letters of Paul,* 2010, Polebridge Press

Ehrman, Bart D., *Heaven and Hell,* 2020, Simon & Schuster

Ehrman, Bart D., *How Jesus Became God,* 2014, HarperCollins

Ehrman, Bart D., *Misquoting Jesus,* 2005, HarperCollins

Ferrell, Lori Anne, *The Bible and the People,* 2008, Yale University Press

Funk, Robert W., Et al., *The Five Gospels,* 1993, Polebridge Press

Funk, Robert W., *The Acts of Jesus,* 1998, Polebridge Press

Hecht, Jennifer Michael. *Doubt,* 2003, HarperCollins

James, William, *Writings:* 1902-1910, 1987, Library of America

Jefferson, Thomas, *The Jefferson Bible,* 1989, Beacon Press

Krieg, Dr. Carl, Essay, *The Birth and Death of the Church in the First Century,* Progressive Christianity**,** November 10, 2022

latimes.com/opinion/story/2021-04-04/christians-heaven-hell-soul

monticello.org/thomas-jefferson/brief-biography-of-jefferson

Nicolson, Adam, *God's Secretaries*, 2003, HarperCollins

Pagels, Elaine, *The Gnostic gospels*, 1979. Vintage Books

Pagels, Elaine, *Why Religion?* 2018, HarperCollins

Peterson, Merrill, editor, *Thomas Jefferson: Writings,* 1984, 2011, Library of America

Pinker, Steven, *Enlightenment Now*, 2018, Penguin Random House

Popper, Karl, *The Open Society and Its Enemies*, 1945, Princeton University Press

Spong, John Shelby, *Reclaiming the Bible for a Non-Religious World*, 2011, HarperOne

Spong, John Shelby, *The Sins of Scripture*, 2005, HarperCollins

Turner, Alice, *The History of Hell*, 1993, Harcourt Brace & Co.

Afterword

If you want to descend into the rabbit hole of scholarly, biblical study, I suggest the following links (especially note the References/Bibliographies):

https://en.wikipedia.org/wiki/New_Testament (Citations: 202; Extensive Bibliography/further Reading)

https://en.wikipedia.org/wiki/Biblical_criticism (References: 203; Further Reading and External Links)

https://en.wikipedia.org/wiki/Jesus_Seminar (References: 86; External Links: 7)

https://www.monticello.org/research-education/thomas-jefferson-encyclopedia/jeffersons-religious-beliefs/ (Reference Links: 31; Further Sources)

https://encyclopediavirginia.org/entries/jefferson-thomas-and-religion/ and

https://encyclopediavirginia.org/entries/virginia-statute-for-establishing-religious-freedom-1786/

Or for a lifetime of Old and New Testament bible study, I suggest:

https://www.amazon.com/HarperCollins-Study-Bible-Revised-Updated/dp/006078685X/ref=sr_1_8?crid=21KOTQHGQ8N10&k

eywords=episcopal+bible+study+guide&qid=1700165191&s=books&sprefix=episcopal+bible%2Cstripbooks%2C355&sr=1-8

https://www.amazon.com/Catholic-Study-Bible-American-4200/dp/0195283899/ref=sr_1_5?crid=2HU29TWTGQJYC&keywords=catholic+study+bible+senior&qid=1700164723&s=books&sprefix=catholic+study+bible+Senior%2Cstripbooks%2C139&sr=1-5

ACKNOWLEDGEMENT

I acknowledge Thomas Jefferson as a genius thinker, writer, innovator, and skeptic. Weighing his personal shortcomings against his contributions to social, political, and religious freedoms that we still enjoy today, he ranks as an all-time great American. To a lesser but important degree, I credit the writings of Karl Popper, agnostic/atheist Bart Ehrman, bible scholars Reza Aslan, John Barton, and the late bishop/believer John Shelby Spong. Those biblical scholars and scores of others over the last 200 years painstakingly examined those same gospels that were troubling to Jefferson. I appreciate, too, the perspective of the intrepid Jesus Seminar (general rule: Beware of finding a Jesus entirely congenial to you). They closely examined the four generally accepted gospels, plus the gospel of Thomas, and agreed by popular vote that about 18 percent of the sayings and 16 percent of the deeds attributed to Jesus in the gospels are authentic. All of the above, I'm sure, appreciate their religious freedom to study, explore, and disagree with conventional beliefs as a consequence of Jefferson's dedication to the separation wall between the church and the state.

I appreciate the patient multiple readings and editing of my wife Carol and initial copyediting of my granddaughter Allyson Bragg. My friend and a Bible fan Michael Diaz, and others read and offered advice on my manuscript, as did Dr. Carl Krieg. All opinions, pearls of wisdom, and flagrant errors, though, are mine alone. I appreciate, too, my departed, holier-than-the-Pope parents, my brothers and sisters, my daughters and their families, and many friends who have all provided life support throughout my endeavors. Thank you all.

About The Author

Thomas (Tom) Huening is a CPA, lawyer, and former carrier-qualified Navy jet fighter pilot and commercial airline pilot.

He has served as a community college Trustee, an elected San Mateo County Supervisor and as the elected County Controller.

See Wikipedia: Tom Huening or SpiritualChoices.com

Books by This Author

The Quintessential Good Samaritan. A biography of John Kelly, who changed the lives of thousands as a devoted Catholic priest, as champion of the poor and father figure to troubled minority youth, and, finally, as a chaplain to San Quentin inmates.

Spiritual Choices: Putting the HERE in Hereafter. An informative and often humorous journey of spiritual enlightenment that spans from Adam and Eve to religion today. Discover choices not revealed by your priest, minister, rabbi, or imam.

Jefferson's Bible - Religious Freedom in America: Do We Agree or Disagree?

With Separation of Church and State?

1. Is Jefferson's wall of separation between church and state important to all religious beliefs or to atheist, agnostic or no religious preference?

2. According to the Declaration of Independence, our Constitution and Bill of Rights, were we founded as a Christian nation?

3. Does it matter if our government dictates a single religious belief? Is it beneficial to have multiple choices of beliefs or non-belief?

4. Do you believe what Jefferson believes, with what your neighbors believe? Is that important to you?

With his Bible?

1. Why did Jefferson feel compelled to write his own version of the Bible?

2. Already in Jefferson's time, historians had uncovered dates and facts about the gospel at odds with Christian dogma. Should we question long-ago church doctrines?

3. Jefferson was raised an Episcopal and tutored by Anglican ministers. What happened?

4. Jefferson believed that the gospels were written by ordinary men reflecting the memories and common wisdom of their time. Do you agree based on what you just read?

5. Jefferson's Bible faults Plato and St. Paul for distorting Jesus's message. Was he justified in his criticism? Does he represent a more accurate Jesus?

6. Do you agree with Jefferson's bible passage choices? With what he left out?

7. Do you believe the biblical research since Jefferson? Does it change your beliefs? We read and accept history as recorded—why not the Bible?

8. Do you believe the miracles in the biblical accounts or maybe miracles in your own life experience?

With the man Jefferson?

1. Politician Jefferson hid his religious views from the public. Why?

2. Jefferson professed belief in "Nature's God." What does that mean to you?

3. As a son of the Enlightenment, did Jefferson rely on reason to the detriment of faith?

4. Jefferson owned slaves. Was he justified because he grew up and lived in Virginia where owning enslaved humans was accepted and common?

5. Jefferson knew that slavery was wrong and should eventually end yet he benefited from his slaves' labor. Could he have been more politically proactive on securing freedom for all?

6. Some say that Jefferson and the founding fathers' failure to deal with slavery led to the Civil War? Do you agree? Did they have a political choice?

7. John F. Kennedy thought that Jefferson was our smartest, best educated president. Do you agree?

8. How would Jefferson's views of separation of church and state play in today's politics?

9. The author presents Jefferson as complicated—good and bad. What do you think?

Made in the USA
Columbia, SC
05 July 2025